Donated by
Friends of
The Woodbridge
Library

DATE DUE

OVERDUE FINE
$0.10 PER DAY

DEMCO

THE ROASTED VEGETABLE

THE ROASTED VEGETABLE

Andrea Chesman

THE HARVARD COMMON PRESS
Boston, Massachusetts

The Harvard Common Press
535 Albany Street
Boston, Massachusetts 02118

www.harvardcommonpress.com

Printed in the United States of America

Printed on acid-free paper

Library of Congress Cataloging-in-Publication Data

Chesman, Andrea.
    The roasted vegetable : how to roast everything from arti-
chokes to zucchini for big, bold flavors in pasta, pizza, risotto,
side dishes, couscous, salsas, dips, sandwiches, and salads / by
Andrea Chesman.
        p. cm.
    ISBN 1-55832-168-3 (hc : alk. paper) — ISBN 1-55832-169-1
(pbk : alk. paper)
        1. Cookery (Vegetables) 2. Roasting (Cookery) I. Title.

TX801.C435 2002
641.6′5—dc21

                                                    2001039593

Special bulk-order discounts are available on this and other
Harvard Common Press books. Companies and organizations
may purchase books for premiums or resale, or may arrange a
custom edition, by contacting the Marketing Director at the
address above.

10 9 8 7 6 5 4 3

Book design by Richard Oriolo
Book illustrations by Linda Hillel

Cover design by Renato Stanisic
Cover photograph by Alexandra Grablewski

CONTENTS

ACKNOWLEDGMENTS

MY DEEPEST APPRECIATION goes to the farmers who grew the vegetables that I have enjoyed so much. My special thanks go to Marian Pollack and Marjorie Susman of Orb Weaver Farm in Monkton, Vermont, and to Will and Judy Stevens of Golden Russet Farm in Shoreham, Vermont. Kira Winslow and Maureen Boksa of the Middlebury Natural Foods Coops were wonderful providers of hard-to-find produce. I thank all the folks at Harvard Common Press for making this book possible. Rory Ruane and Sam Chesman were faithful tasters and kitchen companions, and I am grateful to them for all that they do. Finally, none of this would be possible without the endless support and music. Thanks, Richard.

PREFACE

THIS IS A COOKBOOK FOR VEGETABLE LOVERS—and vegetable haters. It is a cookbook for people who want to eat more vegetables but have had their fill of steamed carrots and stir-fried snow peas. It is for busy people who want to make more delicious vegetable recipes, without fuss and without standing over a hot stove following a complicated recipe. This is a cookbook for people who want to enjoy eating vegetables—lots of vegetables.

When I started writing this book, I didn't know how much it would change the way my family eats. I never envisioned, for example, that my kids would eat roasted green beans as a snack food or that when I roasted green beans, I would need to allow half a pound per person. Now *that* is a serving of vegetables—and a striking contrast to the one steamed broccoli stem that the kids will grudgingly eat.

Roasting vegetables brings out their hidden sweet, nutty flavors—making them extraordinarily appealing and wondrously versatile. This cookbook begins with techniques for very basic roasted vegetables to be served as side dishes. The rest of the book provides recipes for many of the delicious possibilities for combining roasted vegetables with pasta, rice, and greens and for using them on pizzas and in sandwiches, soups, and salads. A final chapter provides recipes for roasting nuts and grains to transform them into delicious granolas and trail mix.

Happy roasting!

ROASTING BASICS:

TECHNIQUES AND EQUIPMENT

THERE IS NOTHING DIFFICULT about roasting vegetables. All you need is an oven to supply heat, a pan in which to spread out the vegetables, some vegetables (of course), and a little oil or butter to encourage browning. It is that simple. Over the course of roasting a few tons of vegetables, however, I have picked up some techniques that guarantee success.

First, a definition of roasting: Roasting is a dry-heat method of cooking. The food is usually cooked at a fairly high temperature in the oven and without the addition of a liquid or sauce. Roasting is quite similar to baking, but generally roasted vegetables are cooked with a light coating of oil or butter, which helps to brown the vegetables and speed the cooking.

All foods lose volume when they are roasted. But since vegetables are mostly water, they lose a great deal of volume. The first time you roast, you may be dismayed by the sheer amount of vegetables being loaded into the oven. Don't worry—they will all cook down. Forkful by forkful, you will eat more vegetables when they have been roasted. This is a good thing, yes?

Equipment

Because you are working with such large volumes of raw vegetables, you will need pans big enough to accommodate them. The pans you use should hold the vegetables in a single layer. If the vegetables are stacked on top of each other, they will steam rather than roast. The texture will be mushy, not tender-crisp, and the flavor will be lacking the caramelized sweetness typical of roasted vegetables.

Most of the recipes specify using a large shallow roasting pan or half sheet pan. Roasting pans come in all sizes; yours should be at least the standard 13 x 16 inches (208 square inches), which easily accommodates a 12-pound roast and fits into most ovens. The sides should be no higher than 2 inches (as opposed to deep roasting pans with 6-inch sides). Even better than a shallow roasting pan is a half sheet pan, which measures 13 x 18 inches (234 square inches). Its 1-inch sides allow for better air circulation. A standard 11 x 17-inch jellyroll pan also can be used. When a single pan is used, it is always placed on a rack in the middle of the oven for even roasting, unless otherwise specified.

What do you do if you don't have a large enough pan? Use two pans and place them side by side in the oven. If the pans do not fit side by side, place one pan on the middle rack and the other on the lower rack and rotate the pans every ten minutes or so. You may have to increase the roasting time slightly.

Lightly oiling the pan before adding the vegetables aids in browning the vegetables, prevents them from sticking to the pan, and eases cleanup. If you prefer, you can substitute nonstick cooking spray for oil.

After the vegetables are cut up, they are usually combined in a large bowl and tossed with oil. A large rubber spatula is the best tool for tossing the vegetables without damaging them. You can use the same spatula to scrape the vegetables out of the bowl and into the roasting pan. For stirring or turning the vegetables as they roast, a metal spatula, or pancake turner, does the best job of getting under the vegetables to move them around.

Techniques

Generally, all the vegetables should be cut to the same size, whether you are dicing (¼- to ⅓-inch dice), slicing (generally ⅜- to ½-inch-thick slices), or cutting into matchsticks (generally ¼-inch-wide strips that are 1½ to 2 inches long). Some vegetables, such as potatoes, may be cut into 1-inch-thick wedges when a crispy outside and a soft inside are desired. Generally, smaller pieces roast better than large ones. I have been served roasted vegetables that have been cut into large chunks, and I have found them unpleasant and unevenly cooked.

The vegetables are usually lightly coated with oil or melted butter, which may or may not be flavored with herbs, spices, or garlic. This fat helps the vegetables to form a crispy outer coating that seals in flavor. The fat also helps the vegetables to brown. I usually prefer to combine the vegetables in a large bowl with the oil and flavoring ingredients because it is easier to coat them evenly this way. But if you prefer, you can combine everything in the roasting pan and toss until the vegetables are evenly coated.

Timing Is Everything

All times in the recipes are approximate. How quickly the vegetables will actually roast depends on many factors: how much water a particular batch of vegetables retains, whether the vegetables are firm and ripe or slightly overripe, how accurate your oven temperature is, how crowded the vegetables are in the pan, whether the pan has a slightly higher or lower rim, and how evenly the vegetables are cut.

Stir the vegetables or shake the pan every ten minutes or so as the vegetables roast. Generally, the vegetables at the edges of the pan will cook more quickly than those in the middle, so stirring is necessary for even cooking. Shaking the pan works best with round vegetables, such as green beans and asparagus. Stirring works best with cubed vegetables, especially large quantities. Use a metal spatula and turn the vegetables over as you stir. Flat rounds and steaks also should be turned over with a metal spatula.

The vegetables are done when they are fork tender, but still juicy, and lightly colored. They should not appear burnt. The flavor of burnt vegetables is acrid and bitter. The flavor of well-roasted vegetables is nutty and sweet. So use your judgment to determine when the vegetables are done, and use the times in the recipes as guidelines.

Ingredients

Vegetables are, of course, the main ingredients in roasted vegetable dishes. Most recipes list a specific vegetable or vegetables to be used. However, the methods are generally applicable to other vegetables as well, so feel free to substitute. I advise using mushrooms sparingly because their flavor tends to dominate. Also, use tomatoes carefully, because they give off so much liquid that the resulting vegetables are very stewlike in character. Usually, the most successful substitutions involve swapping one root vegetable for another or one summer vegetable for another.

The vegetables are almost always lightly coated with melted butter or oil. Most often I use extra virgin olive oil, which comes from the first cold pressing of olives. For roasting, I use a reasonably priced oil and save the really expensive oil for dressing salads. You can substitute other oils, particularly flavored oils. Canola oil and grapeseed oil are good-quality, neutral-tasting oils that can be used for roasting. Oil can be used when a dish is to be served hot, warm, or at room temperature. Butter should be used only when the vegetables are served hot.

Herbs and spices enhance the flavor of many dishes. Try to use fresh herbs, because their flavor is superior to that of dried herbs. In fact, if you have a choice between substituting another fresh herb or using the same herb in dried form, choose the fresh herb. Herbs are another category of ingredients where substitutions are always possible. Feel free to use the fresh herb of your choice in these recipes. Spices should be bought in small quantities and allowed to age for no more than a couple of months in your kitchen. Roasting enhances all the flavor nuances in spices, and that includes the musty off flavors of old spices.

Simple roasted vegetables are often finished with a sprinkling of salt and pepper. If you aren't already a convert to coarse sea salt, try it. It makes a big difference in the final dish.

Roasting Chart

All vegetables, unless otherwise noted, are lightly coated with oil or melted butter before roasting and arranged in a single layer in a shallow roasting pan or half sheet pan. Times are approximate and are very much affected by how crowded the vegetables are in the pan. The vegetables are roasted until they are tender and browned. Salt and pepper, as well as other seasonings, can be applied before or after roasting.

VEGETABLE	INSTRUCTIONS	TIME
Artichokes, baby	Slice in half. Steam until barely tender, 15 minutes. Roast at 425°F.	20 minutes
Asparagus	Roast at 450°F.	15 minutes, depending on thickness
Beans, green or wax	Roast at 500°F.	15 minutes
Beets	Do not peel. Do not coat with oil. Wrap in foil. Roast at 350°F.	Baby beets: 45 to 60 minutes Medium-size beets: 1 to 1¼ hours Large beets: up to 2 hours
Belgian endives	Slice in half. Roast at 450°F.	25 minutes
Bell peppers and chile peppers	Roast under a broiler or over an open flame until well charred, turning to roast evenly. Place in a closed paper or plastic bag for 10 minutes to loosen skins. Peel, seed, and slice.	About 15 minutes
Cabbage, green and red	Cut into 1-inch-wide strips. Roast at 425°F.	20 to 30 minutes
Carrots	Roast at 425°F.	20 to 30 minutes for baby carrots, matchsticks, or slices
Celery root	Roast at 425°F.	30 to 40 minutes for matchsticks or cubes
Corn on the cob	To roast in husks: Peel back husks and remove silks. Fold back husks. Roast at 500°F until lightly browned. Or roast with husks removed. Brushing with oil or butter is optional.	In husks: 20 to 30 minutes With husks removed: 15 minutes
Eggplants	Peel, if desired. Slice ⅜ inch thick. Roast at 400°F, turning once. Or roast whole. Prick in several places before placing in oven.	Slices: 20 to 25 minutes Whole: 40 to 60 minutes
Fennel	Cut into wedges. Roast at 425°F.	15 minutes
Garlic	Slice off top of whole head. Drizzle with a little oil. Cover and roast at 425°F.	45 minutes

VEGETABLE	INSTRUCTIONS	TIME
Jerusalem artichokes	Peel and cut into 1-inch pieces. Roast at 500°F.	15 minutes
Kohlrabi	Peel and cut into matchsticks. Roast at 425°F.	15 minutes
Mushrooms	Slice. Roast at 450°F.	20 to 30 minutes
Okra	Leave whole. Roast at 450°F.	15 minutes
Onions	Roast at 450°F.	¼-inch-thick slices: 20 to 30 minutes Whole pearl: 20 to 30 minutes Whole cipollines: 30 minutes
Parsnips	Peel and slice ½ inch thick. Roast at 425°F.	30 minutes
Potatoes, baking	Peel, if desired. Cut into wedges. Roast at 425°F, turning once.	20 minutes
Potatoes, new	Cut in half. Roast at 425°F.	25 to 40 minutes, depending on size
Rutabagas	Peel and cut into 1-inch cubes. Roast at 450°F.	35 minutes
Shallots	Cut into quarters. Roast at 425°F.	30 minutes
Squash, summer (yellow and zucchini)	Roast at 450°F.	Baby halves and ½-inch-thick slices: 15 minutes
Squash, winter	Peel and cut into wedges, ½-inch-thick slices, or ⅓-inch dice. Roast at 350° to 375°F, turning slices or wedges once, or stirring dice occasionally.	20 to 30 minutes
Sweet potatoes	Peel, if desired. Cut into wedges. Roast at 500°F, turning once.	15 to 20 minutes
Tomatillos	Peel the papery skin, rinse, and pat dry. Roast at 425°F.	15 minutes
Tomatoes	Cut in half and drizzle with oil. Roast at 425°F.	30 to 45 minutes, to serve as side dish 1¼ to 1½ hours, to make thick sauce
Tomatoes, cherry	Leave whole. Roast at 425°F.	20 minutes
Turnips	Peel and cut into 1-inch cubes. Roast at 425°F.	About 25 minutes

SIMPLY VEGETABLES: SIDE DISHES

Roasted Baby Artichokes with Aioli

Simply the Best Roasted Asparagus

Lemon-Roasted Asparagus

Sesame-Roasted Asparagus

World's Best Green Beans

Soy-Roasted Green Beans

Gingered Roasted Beets

Dilled Roasted Cabbage

Sweet-and-Sour Red Cabbage

Herb-and-Honey-Roasted Baby Carrots

Glazed Carrot Coins

Roasted Corn on the Cob

Quick Roasted Corn

Roasted Corn Cakes

Roasted Eggplant with Tomato-Basil Relish

Soy-Glazed Eggplant

Roasted Endives

Roasted Fennel Wedges

Garlic Puree

Roasted Garlic

Roasted Kohlrabi

Crisp Roasted Jerusalem Artichokes

Roasted Leeks

Roasted Portobello Caps

Mixed Roasted Mushrooms in a Soy Vinaigrette

Roasted Okra

Oven-Fried Okra

Roasted Onion Slices

Caramelized Cipollines

Roasted Parsnip Chips

Roasted Peppers

Roasted New Potatoes with Garlic and Herbs

Roasted Potatoes and Celery Root

Oven-Roasted Fries

Crispy Smashed Potatoes

Roasted Shallot Confit

Maple-Glazed Rutabagas

Herbed Summer Squash

Zucchini Chips with Feta and Herbs

Cider-Glazed Acorn Squash

Honey-Roasted Delicata Squash Rings

Bejeweled Squash Cubes

Spaghetti Squash with Tomato-Garlic Confit

Spicy Sweet Potato Wedges

Garlicky Sweet Potatoes

Roasted Whole Cherry Tomatoes

Slow-Roasted Rice-Stuffed Tomatoes

Roasted Tomato Sauce

Lemon-Garlic Summer Vegetables

Summer Vegetable Gratin

Herb-Roasted Root Vegetables

Roasted Baby Artichokes with Aioli

NOT ALL ARTICHOKES are created equal. Some are actually quite tough. So don't be at all shy about peeling off the outer leaves until you are left with just tender inner leaves. Baby artichokes make a beautiful presentation because they have no "choke." You can find recipes for roasted artichokes that do not require steaming first, but I find the steaming necessary to prevent the artichokes from becoming too dry. So why roast at all? Because roasting brings out a nutty, sweet flavor that would otherwise be missed. The aioli—that heavenly garlicky mayonnaise—is optional but highly recommended.

Juice of 1 lemon
12 baby artichokes (about ¾ pound)
2 tablespoons extra virgin olive oil
2 tablespoons chopped fresh thyme leaves
Salt and freshly ground black pepper
Aioli (recipe follows)

1. Fill a large bowl with water and add the lemon juice. Prepare the artichokes one at a time so they do not discolor. First, pull off the outer leaves and discard. With a paring knife, trim the stem, keeping it as long as possible. Using kitchen scissors, cut off the prickly leaf tips. With a large knife, cut the artichokes in half vertically and place in the water.

2. Steam the artichokes over boiling water until just barely tender, about 15 minutes.

3. Meanwhile, preheat the oven to 425°F. Lightly oil a baking sheet large enough to hold the artichokes in a single layer.

4. In a large bowl, toss the artichokes with the oil and thyme. Season with salt and pepper to taste. Arrange in a single layer on the baking sheet.

5. Roast for about 20 minutes, until the artichokes are completely tender and beginning to brown on the edges, stirring or shaking the pan occasionally for even cooking.

6. Serve warm or at room temperature, passing the aioli at the table.

Aioli

6 garlic cloves

2 large egg yolks

Juice of 1 lemon

1 teaspoon Dijon mustard

Salt and white pepper

1 cup pure olive oil, or ½ cup peanut oil and ½ cup extra virgin olive oil

1. In a food processor or blender, process the garlic until pureed. Whisk the egg yolks in a small bowl until smooth and add to the garlic, along with the lemon juice, mustard, and salt and pepper to taste. Process until smooth.

2. With the machine running, very slowly pour in the oil in a slow, steady stream. Let the machine run until you have a thick, shiny sauce.

3. Serve at once or cover and refrigerate for up to 4 hours.

Aioli Notes Whenever you cook with raw eggs, as in aioli, there is a small risk of salmonella. So use the freshest eggs possible and store them at temperatures below 40°F. Serve the aioli immediately or hold it in the refrigerator for no more than a few hours. If you are serving it to children, elderly people, or anyone with a compromised immune system, consider using pasteurized eggs instead of fresh eggs. Or make a sauce using store-bought mayonnaise doctored up with minced fresh garlic and freshly squeezed lemon juice.

Simply the Best Roasted Asparagus

SERVES 4

SOMETIMES LESS IS MORE, and that is definitely the case when cooking fresh, locally grown asparagus. It's all very well to have asparagus in the market year-round, but asparagus shipped from another corner of the globe is no better than strawberries shipped halfway around the world—pretty to look at but lacking in flavor. Save this simple, unadorned treatment for fresh, in-season asparagus that needs no flavor enhancements. This asparagus isn't that pretty to look at, but it is wonderful to eat. For roasting, choose medium-thick spears over pencil-thin ones.

1 pound asparagus (12 to 16 medium-thick spears), bottoms trimmed
2 tablespoons extra virgin olive oil
Coarse sea salt or kosher salt

1. Preheat the oven to 450°F. Lightly oil a large shallow roasting pan or half sheet pan.

2. Arrange the asparagus in a single, uncrowded layer in the pan. Drizzle the oil over the asparagus and roll to coat evenly.

3. Roast for about 15 minutes, until the asparagus is lightly browned, shaking the pan occasionally for even cooking.

4. Transfer the asparagus to a serving platter and sprinkle with salt to taste. Serve immediately.

Lemon-Roasted Asparagus

SERVES 4

WHEN YOU WANT to add an extra spark to asparagus, lemon juice and chopped fresh herbs are the perfect enhancements. If you have a choice, medium-thick spears work better than thin ones.

1 pound asparagus (12 to 16 medium-thick spears), bottoms trimmed

2 tablespoons extra virgin olive oil or butter, melted

2 tablespoons freshly squeezed lemon juice

Salt and freshly ground black pepper

1. Preheat the oven to 400°F.

2. Arrange the asparagus in a single layer in a large shallow roasting pan or half sheet pan. Drizzle the oil or butter and lemon juice over the asparagus and roll to coat evenly. Season generously with salt and pepper.

3. Roast for about 15 minutes, until the asparagus is tender and lightly browned.

4. Serve hot.

Herb-Roasted Asparagus: **Substitute red or white wine vinegar and 1 tablespoon chopped fresh herbs for the lemon juice.**

Peeling Asparagus Many cooks swear that asparagus should always be peeled. I think it is unnecessary with absolutely fresh asparagus, but peeling can be a great tenderizer for older stems. To peel, use a swivel-bladed vegetable peeler and strip away just a thin layer all the way around the stem, starting about an inch or two below the tip. The woody bottoms of the asparagus should be cut off and discarded.

Sesame-Roasted Asparagus

SERVES 4

TRADITIONAL CHINESE-STYLE dishes are usually stir-fried, not roasted. But roasting bakes the flavor into the asparagus, making for a deeply satisfying dish. This asparagus makes a fine accompaniment to fried rice or lo mein.

2 tablespoons oyster sauce (see Note)

2 tablespoons rice wine or dry sherry

1 tablespoon toasted sesame oil

1 tablespoon peanut oil

1 pound asparagus (12 to 16 medium-thick spears), bottoms trimmed

2 tablespoons white (hulled) sesame seeds

1. Preheat the oven to 400°F. Lightly oil a large shallow roasting or half sheet pan.

2. In a small bowl, combine the oyster sauce, rice wine, and oils.

3. Arrange the asparagus in a single layer in the pan. Pour the sauce over the asparagus and roll to coat evenly.

4. Roast for 10 minutes. Shake the pan, sprinkle with the sesame seeds, and roast for another 5 minutes, until the asparagus is tender and lightly browned.

5. Serve hot.

Note: **Oyster sauce is found wherever Chinese foods are sold. Not all oyster sauces are derived from oysters, but most do contain some form of fish extract. You may find bottles labeled with the oxymoronic "vegetarian oyster sauce," which do not contain any fish extract.**

World's Best Green Beans

SERVES 4 TO 6

I LOVE THESE green beans! Everyone loves these green beans—even though they are not the prettiest vegetables I have ever served. When I make them, I can count on at least half disappearing before I get the bowl to the table. Once you try one, you will want to eat more. We enjoy them as a side dish, snack, or hors d'oeuvre. All gardeners should have this recipe in their repertoires, because it calls for a huge pile of green beans and leaves the family clamoring for more.

2 pounds green beans, ends trimmed
2 tablespoons extra virgin olive oil
Coarse sea salt or kosher salt

1. Preheat the oven to 500°F. Lightly oil a large shallow roasting or half sheet pan.

2. Arrange the green beans in a single, uncrowded layer in the pan. Drizzle the oil over the beans and roll until evenly coated.

3. Roast for about 15 minutes, until the beans are well browned, shaking the pan occasionally for even cooking.

4. Transfer the beans to a serving bowl and sprinkle with salt to taste. Serve immediately.

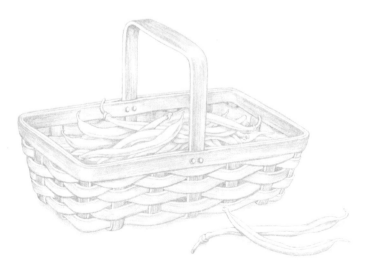

Soy-Roasted Green Beans

SERVES 4 TO 6

THESE BEANS NICELY complement an Asian-inspired menu, and they can be roasting in the oven while the wok is occupied with a stir-fry. But do not limit yourself to nights when you are making a stir-fry; these beans are tasty anytime.

2 tablespoons toasted sesame oil
2 tablespoons soy sauce
1 tablespoon rice wine or dry sherry
2 garlic cloves, minced
2 pounds green beans, ends trimmed
Freshly ground black pepper

1. Preheat the oven to 450°F. Lightly oil a large shallow roasting or half sheet pan.

2. In a small bowl, combine the sesame oil, soy sauce, rice wine, and garlic.

3. Arrange the green beans in a single, uncrowded layer in the pan. Drizzle the sauce over the beans and roll until evenly coated.

4. Roast for about 15 minutes, until the beans are well browned, shaking the pan occasionally for even cooking.

5. Transfer the beans to a serving bowl and season with pepper to taste. Serve immediately.

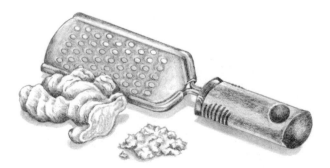

Gingered Roasted Beets

SERVES 6 TO 8

A WONDERFUL MAKE-AHEAD dish for Thanksgiving, these flavorful beets are cloaked in a delicate ginger syrup. They can be served warm, at room temperature, or chilled.

4 to 6 medium-size beets (about 1½ pounds), tops and roots trimmed to 1 inch

1 cup cider vinegar

1 cup water

½ cup sugar

One 2-inch piece fresh ginger, peeled and sliced

2 garlic cloves, sliced

½ teaspoon salt

Freshly ground black pepper

1. Preheat the oven to 350°F.

2. Wash the beets, but do not peel. Place on a large sheet of heavy-duty aluminum foil and wrap to form a well-sealed packet. Or place in a baking dish and cover.

3. Roast for about 1¼ hours, until tender; adjust the time for larger or smaller beets. The beets are done when they are easily pierced with a fork. Let cool, covered.

4. Meanwhile, combine the vinegar, water, sugar, ginger, garlic, and salt in a medium-size nonreactive saucepan. Simmer over low heat for about 10 minutes, until syrupy. Pour into a large bowl and let cool.

5. Peel the beets and cut into thin wedges. Add to the syrup and season with pepper to taste. Stir to coat. Cover and marinate in the refrigerator overnight.

6. Remove the ginger and garlic, and serve.

Good Old Roasted Beets You don't need to put roasted beets in a syrup or sauce to enjoy them. Just wrap the beets in foil and roast until tender (1 to 1¼ hours for medium-size beets). Serve peeled or unpeeled.

Dilled Roasted Cabbage

THIS HUMBLE DISH comes with delicious possibilities. Enjoy it as a simple peasant dish, or add the optional sour cream and transform it into something more luxurious. Or serve it on a bed of mashed potatoes—an uncommonly tasty version of colcannon.

1 small head green cabbage (about 2 pounds), quartered, cored, and cut into ½ -inch-wide strips
¼ cup (½ stick) butter, melted
2 teaspoons dill seeds
Salt and freshly ground black pepper
Sour cream (optional)

1. Preheat the oven to 425°F. Lightly oil a large shallow roasting or half sheet pan.

2. In a large bowl, combine the cabbage and butter. Toss to coat. Arrange in a shallow layer in the pan.

3. Roast for 20 to 25 minutes, until the cabbage is very lightly browned and tender, stirring occasionally for even cooking. Do not let the cabbage burn, or it will taste bitter.

4. Transfer the cabbage to a serving bowl. Add the dill seeds and season generously with salt and pepper. Serve hot, passing the sour cream at the table, if desired.

Colcannon: **Omit the dill seeds and stir in ½ cup chopped scallions (white and tender green parts only). Serve the cabbage on a bed of boiled potatoes mashed with plenty of butter and whole milk or half-and-half.**

Sweet-and-Sour Red Cabbage

SERVES 4 TO 6

A CLASSIC FALL harvest dish. The vinegar helps preserve the vibrant color of this gorgeous vegetable.

1 small head red cabbage (about 2 pounds), quartered, cored, and cut into ½-inch-wide strips

1 large onion, sliced

2 tart apples, such as Granny Smith, peeled, cored, halved, and sliced ¼ inch thick

3 tablespoons canola oil

1 tablespoon caraway seeds, or to taste

1 teaspoon ground allspice, or to taste

Salt and freshly ground black pepper

¼ cup firmly packed light brown sugar, or to taste

3 tablespoons cider vinegar, or to taste

1. Preheat the oven to 425°F. Lightly oil a large shallow roasting or half sheet pan.

2. In a large bowl, combine the cabbage, onion, and apples. Add the oil, caraway seeds, allspice, and salt and pepper to taste. Toss to coat. Arrange in a single layer in the pan. Do not wash the bowl.

3. Roast for about 30 minutes, until browned and tender, stirring occasionally for even cooking.

4. Return the roasted cabbage mixture to the bowl. Add the brown sugar and vinegar. Toss to mix. Taste and adjust the seasonings, adding more brown sugar, vinegar, allspice, caraway, or salt and pepper as needed.

5. Transfer to a serving bowl and serve hot.

Herb-and-Honey-Roasted Baby Carrots

SERVES 4

MOST PEOPLE WILL SAY they prefer raw carrots to cooked ones, but that is usually because they have had only carrots that have been steamed or boiled—methods that drain away the sweet carrot flavor. Roasting is perfect for carrots because it intensifies their sweetness while making them tender.

1 pound baby carrots

1 teaspoon chopped fresh thyme or rosemary leaves

Salt and freshly ground black pepper

2 tablespoons extra virgin olive oil or butter, melted

1 tablespoon honey

1. Preheat the oven to 425°F. Lightly oil a baking pan large enough to hold the carrots in a single layer.

2. Arrange the carrots in a single layer in the pan. Sprinkle the thyme or rosemary and salt and pepper to taste over the carrots. Drizzle the oil over the carrots and roll to evenly coat.

3. Roast for 15 to 20 minutes, until the carrots are mostly tender when pierced with a fork, stirring or shaking the pan occasionally for even cooking. Drizzle with the honey. Return to the oven for another 5 to 10 minutes to finish roasting. Watch carefully and do not let the carrots burn.

4. Serve hot.

Glazed Carrot Coins

PLEASE DON'T OVERCOOK the carrots! They should be roasted to a tender, not mushy, state.

1½ pounds carrots, sliced into ½-inch-thick rounds

2 tablespoons butter, melted

3 tablespoons freshly squeezed orange juice

1 tablespoon pure maple syrup

2 teaspoons peeled and grated fresh ginger

Pinch of nutmeg

Salt and freshly ground black pepper

1. Preheat the oven to 425°F. Lightly oil a baking pan just large enough to hold the carrots in a single layer.

2. Transfer the carrots to the pan. Drizzle the butter over the carrots and toss to coat. Arrange in a single layer.

3. Roast for about 10 minutes. Meanwhile, combine the orange juice, maple syrup, ginger, nutmeg, and salt and pepper to taste in a small bowl.

4. Remove the carrots from the oven and pour the glaze over them. With a metal spatula, turn the carrots over. Roast for another 15 minutes, until the carrots are lightly browned and easily pierced with a fork. Stir with the spatula to coat the carrots with the glaze on the bottom of the pan.

5. Serve hot.

Roasted Corn on the Cob

SERVES 4 TO 8

SWEET CORN IS MADE even sweeter by roasting. This is probably the most flavorful way to cook corn, although it may not be the best method to use during the dog days of August. If you can still find fresh sweet corn in September as the weather cools, you must try this method. Roasted corn is similar to grilled corn, but the kernels remain juicy, and the flavor is not masked by smoke.

8 ears corn
Salt and freshly ground black pepper
Butter (optional)

1. Preheat the oven to 500°F.

2. Peel back the husks of the corn and remove the inner silks. Then fold the husks back over the corn, smoothing them into place. They will fit loosely, leaving the tips of the ears exposed.

3. Place directly on the oven rack and roast for 20 to 30 minutes, until the corn is lightly browned, turning occasionally.

4. Remove the husks. It is a good idea to wear oven mitts and to work over a large bowl or newspaper to catch the crumbling husks.

5. Serve at once, passing the salt, pepper mill, and butter at the table.

A Small Cleanup Problem Roasting corn with the husks on does result in a small amount of litter at the bottom of the oven—the husks will dry up and crumble as you turn the ears. Just wait until the oven cools, then remove the lower rack and brush out the husks with a whisk broom.

Quick Roasted Corn

SERVES 4 TO 8

ALTHOUGH IT IS PREFERABLE to roast corn in its husks for the best flavor, you can roast corn that has already been shucked. I find this method especially convenient if I am using the corn in another dish, such as a salsa, where the flavor is a little less important than if you are eating the corn out of hand.

8 ears corn
Extra virgin olive oil or butter, melted (optional)
Salt and freshly ground black pepper (optional)
Butter (optional)

1. Preheat the oven to 500°F.

2. Brush the corn with oil, if using. Arrange in a single layer on a baking sheet.

3. Roast for 15 to 20 minutes, until the corn is lightly browned, turning occasionally for even cooking.

4. Serve at once, passing the salt, pepper mill, and butter, if using, at the table.

Roasted Corn Cakes

SERVES 4 TO 6

SIDE DISH OR BREAKFAST—your choice. If you serve these for breakfast, be sure to pass maple syrup at the table. The recipe provides roasting instructions, but you can use any leftover roasted corn.

4 ears corn, husks removed

1½ cups corn flour or finely ground cornmeal

2 teaspoons baking powder

½ teaspoon salt

2 large eggs, separated

1 tablespoon honey

1 cup milk

¼ cup (½ stick) butter, melted

Oil for griddle

1. Preheat the oven to 500°F.

2. Arrange the corn in a single layer on a baking sheet. Roast for 15 to 20 minutes, until the corn is browned, turning occasionally for even cooking. Set aside to cool. Reduce the oven temperature to 200°F.

3. Meanwhile, in a medium-size bowl, combine the corn flour, baking powder, and salt. Whisk to mix well.

4. In another medium-size bowl, combine the egg yolks, honey, milk, and butter. Whisk to combine. Strip the corn kernels from the cobs and add to the egg mixture. Add the corn flour mixture and stir just enough to combine.

5. In a clean medium-size bowl, beat the egg whites until they form soft peaks. Fold into the corn batter.

6. Heat a griddle over medium-high heat. Lightly oil the griddle. Spoon the batter onto the hot griddle to make 4-inch cakes, using about ¼ cup batter per cake. Cook until lightly browned, then flip and cook until lightly browned on the other side, about 5 minutes total. Keep warm in the oven while you continue to make the cakes until all the batter is used.

7. Serve warm.

Roasted Eggplant with Tomato-Basil Relish

SERVES 4 TO 6

EGGPLANT IS AN AGREEABLE candidate for roasting—very willing to absorb flavors from the oil it is brushed with. The only trick is to slice it evenly and to a thickness of about ⅜ inch. If you slice it thicker, it will dry out as it roasts, becoming rubbery rather than juicy. If you slice it thinner, it will char and become brittle.

TOMATO-BASIL RELISH

2 large ripe tomatoes, cored, seeded, and diced

2 scallions, white and tender green parts only, finely chopped

2 tablespoons finely chopped fresh basil leaves

2 tablespoons extra virgin olive oil

1 tablespoon sherry or red wine vinegar, or more to taste

Salt and freshly ground black pepper

EGGPLANT

2 tablespoons extra virgin olive oil

2 garlic cloves, minced

Salt and freshly ground black pepper

1 large or 2 small eggplants (about 2 pounds), peeled and sliced into ⅜-inch-thick rounds

1. To make the relish, combine the tomatoes, scallions, basil, oil, and sherry in a medium-size bowl. Season generously with salt and pepper. Taste and adjust the seasonings, adding more vinegar, salt, or pepper as needed. Cover and set aside at room temperature.

2. Preheat the oven to 400°F. Lightly oil a large shallow roasting or half sheet pan.

3. To make the eggplant, combine the oil and garlic in a small bowl. Season generously with salt and pepper. Brush both sides of the eggplant slices with the seasoned oil. Arrange in a single layer in the pan.

4. Roast for 20 to 25 minutes, until the eggplant is well browned and very tender, turning once.

5. To serve, divide the eggplant among four to six plates and spoon a couple of tablespoons of the relish on top. Pass any additional relish at the table.

Soy-Glazed Eggplant

SERVES 4

LARGE, PURPLE ITALIAN eggplants were once our only choice when it came to this flavor-absorbing vegetable. But today we have a wide selection. Look for lavender Chinese eggplants; narrow, thin-skinned French eggplants; and Japanese eggplants, which look a lot like baby Italian eggplants. Recently I have seen egg-shaped, white eggplants and round, orange ones. This recipe is wonderful with eggplants of any size and shape, but it's best with small eggplants that can be served in halves.

8 small (4- to 6-ounce) eggplants

¼ cup soy sauce

2 tablespoons rice wine or dry sherry

2 tablespoons toasted sesame oil

4 garlic cloves, minced

2 tablespoons peeled and minced fresh ginger

1 tablespoon sugar

2 to 4 tablespoons white (hulled) sesame seeds

1. To prepare the eggplants, trim off the stem ends. Cut each in half lengthwise. Score the flesh of each half into a diamond pattern, cutting almost to the skin. Place skin side down in a baking pan just large enough to hold the eggplant snugly in a single layer.

2. In a small bowl, combine the soy sauce, rice wine, sesame oil, garlic, ginger, and sugar. Pour the glaze over the eggplant and gently massage it into the flesh. Let stand while you preheat the oven, or hold for up to 8 hours in the refrigerator.

3. Preheat the oven to 450°F.

4. Turn the eggplant cut side down and roast for 10 minutes. Carefully turn the eggplant again, using a metal spatula to loosen the flesh from the pan, if needed. Roast for another 10 minutes. Sprinkle with the sesame seeds and continue roasting for about 5 minutes more, until the seeds are lightly colored and the eggplant is tender throughout.

5. Serve warm or at room temperature.

Eggplant Buying Tips There are hundreds of varieties of eggplants, all having originated from the plant that grows wild throughout Southeast Asia and India. If you go to a specialty food store or a farmers' market, you are likely to see eggplants that look like eggs, as well as ones that are orange, lavender, white, or tinged with rose. When grown under ideal conditions, they undoubtedly differ in flavor, degree of bitterness, and tenderness of skin. Unfortunately, you can't tell whether an eggplant has been well treated by weather and growing conditions, so these differences may not be apparent.

Most often you will see large, bulbous, dark purple American eggplants. Italian eggplants have the same color as American but are longer and thinner. At my supermarket, both are labeled "Italian eggplant," and you are never sure which one is in the bin. Long, thin, lavender eggplants are usually called Chinese eggplants. They have very mild (not bitter) flesh, small seeds, and tender skin. Japanese eggplants are smaller than Chinese and are dark purple like American eggplants.

Whichever variety you buy, look for glossy skin without bruises or soft spots. An eggplant should feel heavy for its size. Choose smaller rather than larger eggplants. Overgrown, overmature eggplants are more likely to have a bitter flavor.

Eggplant Roasting Tricks Eggplant has a miserable tendency to absorb oil, and unless there is some oil on the surface, it won't brown nicely. I have found that eggplant sliced ⅜ inch thick is ideal for both roasting and grilling. Brush the slices with oil just before placing them in the oven. The ideal roasted eggplant slice is well browned and slightly crusty outside and moist and juicy inside.

Roasted Endives

OFTEN TREATED AS a salad vegetable, Belgian endives—or witloof chicory, as they are also called—are wonderfully suited to roasting, which brings out their essentially sweet character. Break out a bottle of the best vinegar you have on hand for this exquisitely simple dish.

8 Belgian endives
2 tablespoons extra virgin olive oil
High-quality balsamic, sherry, tarragon, or any herb vinegar
Coarse sea salt or kosher salt and freshly ground black pepper

1. Preheat the oven to 450°F. Lightly oil a baking dish just large enough to hold the endives in a single layer.

2. Carefully trim the root end of each endive to remove any bad spots or rough edges, but do not remove. Cut each endive in half lengthwise. Brush with the oil and arrange cut side up in a single layer in the pan.

3. Roast for about 25 minutes, until the endives are tender and lightly browned.

4. Transfer to a serving bowl or platter. Drizzle vinegar over the endives and sprinkle with salt and pepper to taste. Serve hot or at room temperature.

Roasted Fennel Wedges

SERVES 4

FOR FENNEL LOVERS ONLY! Some people prefer fennel as an accent vegetable—that is, served in small quantities. Others appreciate how the roasting process brings out the anise flavor of this distinctive vegetable.

4 fennel bulbs, trimmed and cut into wedges, stalks discarded
Extra virgin olive oil
High-quality balsamic vinegar
Salt and freshly ground black pepper

1. Preheat the oven to 425°F.

2. Brush the fennel with the oil and arrange in a single layer on a baking sheet.

3. Roast for 15 minutes, until the wedges are tender and beginning to brown on the edges.

4. Transfer the fennel to a serving bowl or platter. Drizzle a little vinegar over the fennel and sprinkle with salt and pepper to taste. Serve warm or at room temperature.

In Praise of Balsamic Vinegar A few drops of high-quality balsamic vinegar over a serving of roasted vegetables works magic. Its intensely woody and fragrant flavor matches the nutty sweetness of the caramelized vegetables perfectly. Traditionally made balsamic vinegar has been aged for more than fifteen years in wooden casks and can cost more than fifty dollars a pint. If you can find it and you can afford it, great. If not, most specialty food stores carry balsamic vinegar that has been aged for at least three years and costs about twelve dollars a pint. Any vegetable can be lightly coated with extra virgin olive oil, roasted until lightly browned, and then sprinkled with a little balsamic vinegar and salt and pepper: simple and delicious.

Garlic Puree

YOU HAVE BECOME hopelessly addicted to the seductive flavor of roasted garlic. You must have it on your toast, on your corn, in your pasta sauce, and on your steamed green beans. What to do? Make this simple puree and keep it on hand for whenever you need it. Use it extravagantly—like a basic black dress, it goes with almost everything.

12 heads garlic
½ cup plus 1 tablespoon extra virgin olive oil
Salt and freshly ground black pepper

1. Preheat the oven to 425°F.

2. Remove the outer papery covering of the garlic. Slice off the top of each head so most of the cloves are exposed. Place on a large square of aluminum foil for easy cleanup, or select the smallest baking dish you have that can hold the heads in a single layer. Drizzle 1 teaspoon of the oil over each head. Fold the foil over the heads to completely enclosed them, or cover the baking dish with foil.

3. Roast for about 45 minutes, until the garlic is completely soft.

4. When cool enough to handle, squeeze the garlic pulp into a small bowl. Mash with a fork. Stir in ¼ cup of the oil. Season with salt and pepper to taste.

5. Scrape the garlic into a small, airtight container with a lid. Smooth the top of the puree and pour the remaining 1 tablespoon oil over the top to seal out any air.

6. Store in the refrigerator for up to several months. After using some puree, top it off with more oil as needed.

The Many Ways to Enjoy Roasted Garlic Roasting mellows the flavor of raw garlic, which may explain roasted garlic's newfound popularity. Here are some ideas for using it.

- Add it as a seasoning to soups, salad dressings, and pasta sauces.
- Serve it alongside baked potatoes, or mix it into sour cream for a topping.
- Spread it on bruschetta.
- Serve it with fresh bread and high-quality extra virgin olive oil. Let your guests dip the bread in the oil, then smear the bread with the garlic.
- Spread it on pizza dough before topping with sauce.
- Instead of roasting vegetables with slivered or crushed garlic, simply toss the roasted vegetables with a teaspoon of garlic puree—adding the garlic flavor without the risk of burning the garlic.

Roasted Garlic

ROASTED GARLIC IS EVERYWHERE these days—in crackers, cheese, salad dressings, and pasta sauces. This is where it all begins. You can multiply this recipe to make as much as you need. Each head will yield about 1 heaping tablespoon of puree. A great way to serve roasted garlic is as an accompaniment to bread. Offer the roasted cloves in one small dish and a high-quality extra virgin olive oil in another. Diners can dip the bread in olive oil, then smear a clove of garlic on it. Heavenly!

1 head garlic
1 teaspoon extra virgin olive oil

1. Preheat the oven to 425°F.

2. Remove the outer papery covering of the garlic. Slice off the top of the head so most of the cloves are exposed. Place on a square of aluminum foil for easy cleanup, or select the smallest baking dish you have. Drizzle the oil over the cloves. Fold the foil over the head to completely enclose it, or cover the baking dish with foil.

3. Roast for about 45 minutes, until the garlic is completely soft and lightly browned.

4. To serve, separate the head into individual cloves. Allow your guests to squeeze out the softened garlic as needed. Or squeeze out the cloves into a small serving dish. If you have leftovers, squeeze out the pulp into a small dish, cover with olive oil, and store, tightly covered, in the refrigerator for up to 1 month.

Roasted Kohlrabi

THIS VEGETABLE IS straight out of *The X-Files*—it looks like a spaceship that has sprouted leaves, and it has a mostly cult following. Raw, it tastes like a cross between celery and apple. Roasted, it tastes like a mild, sweet turnip and is just plain delicious. You can substitute kohlrabi in any recipe that calls for turnip.

4 medium-size to large kohlrabies
3 tablespoons extra virgin olive oil
Salt and freshly ground black pepper

1. Preheat the oven to 425°F. Lightly oil a large shallow roasting or half sheet pan.

2. To prepare the kohlrabies, trim the root ends and the stems that sprout from the bulbs. Peel the bulbs and cut into matchsticks. Transfer to a large bowl, add the oil, and toss to coat. Arrange in a single layer in the pan.

3. Roast for about 15 minutes, until the kohlrabi is tender and lightly browned. Watch carefully so that it does not burn.

4. Transfer the kohlrabi to a serving plate or bowl. Sprinkle with salt and pepper to taste and serve hot.

Crisp Roasted Jerusalem Artichokes

SERVES 4

NATIVE AMERICAN SUNFLOWERS produce edible tubers that taste like a cross between potatoes and artichokes. Roasting brings out their natural sweetness, and roasting in a nut oil underscores their nutty flavor. This is probably the best way to prepare these little-appreciated morsels. Peeling is optional, but I prefer them that way. Buy 2 pounds of "sunchokes," use a sharp paring knife, and don't worry about paring away the small, hard-to-peel knobs.

1 to 2 pounds Jerusalem artichokes
2 tablespoons walnut, peanut, hazelnut, or extra virgin olive oil
Coarse sea salt or kosher salt and freshly ground black pepper

1. Preheat the oven to 500°F. Lightly oil a baking dish or sheet pan large enough to hold the Jerusalem artichokes in a single layer.

2. Peel the Jerusalem artichokes or scrub them well. Cut into 1-inch pieces and brush with the oil. Arrange in a single layer in the pan.

3. Roast for about 15 minutes, until the chokes are tender and well browned, shaking the pan occasionally for even cooking. Shake the pan more frequently toward the end of the roasting time, as they will go from well browned to burnt rather quickly.

4. Transfer the chokes to a serving bowl or platter. Sprinkle with salt and pepper to taste and serve at once.

A Dainty Morsel by Any Name If you haven't tried roasted Jerusalem artichokes, you are missing out on a real treat. These native American sunflowers have nothing to do with either Jerusalem or artichokes. The name is a corruption of the Italian *girasola articiocco*, or "sunflower artichoke." *Girasola* means "turning to the sun," which is what sunflowers do as they grow. You will sometimes find these tubers marketed under the name sunchokes. They look rather like gingerroot.

Under any name, these knobby tubers are a treat—starchy like potatoes, but much sweeter, with a subtle nutty flavor. They can be sliced or grated raw for salads, but they develop their best flavor when roasted. Nutritionally, they are a good source of iron and niacin and are exceptionally low in calories (about 60 calories in a half cup of raw slices).

You can find Jerusalem artichokes year-round, but they tend to be harvested in late fall where winters are harsh, and in late spring where winters are mild enough to allow them to winter over in the ground. Select the smoothest firm tubers you can find. They should be free of discoloration or mold. Store in perforated plastic bags in the refrigerator for up to 2 weeks.

Jerusalem artichokes are incredibly easy to grow. Just clear a patch of land—not in your vegetable or flower garden, because these plants are invasive and prolific and will take over your garden if you are not careful. They make a great hedgerow. Plant in late fall where winters are harsh or very early spring (no later than February). Set the tubers in rows about 6 inches deep and 18 inches apart. They need a long growing season to flower but will produce tubers even if they do not flower. In my Vermont garden, they bloom in late September or early October, as long as there has not been a killing frost. Cut the plants down when the leaves are decayed and dig up the tubers as needed.

Roasted Leeks

TECHNICALLY, THESE LEEKS are braised, not roasted. But who can complain about technicalities when the results are so meltingly tender and delicious? Dry-roasting leeks is okay when the leeks are sliced and are part of a mix of vegetables. For leeks to be enjoyed on their own, however, they must be tamed with a little braising liquid.

8 small to medium-size leeks, white parts only, trimmed
2 tablespoons extra virgin olive oil
1 cup high-quality neutral-tasting chicken or vegetable broth
Salt and freshly ground black pepper

1. Preheat the oven to 425°F. Lightly oil a 9 x 13-inch baking dish.

2. Brush the oil on the leeks and arrange in a single layer in the dish.

3. Roast for about 20 minutes, shaking the dish occasionally for even cooking. Add the broth and roast for another 10 minutes.

4. Transfer the leeks to a serving platter. Sprinkle with salt and pepper to taste and serve hot or at room temperature.

Washing Leeks Leeks often harbor quite a bit of dirt between their leaves. To prepare a leek, first cut away the tough green top. Peel off any tough outer leaves. Trim off the root end. Make a long vertical slit through the center of the leek or cut it in half vertically. Wash under cold running water, flipping through the leaves to expose the inner surfaces to the water. Pat dry.

If you are slicing the leeks anyway, you can do so before washing. To wash, immerse the slices in a bowl of water. Swish the slices, then let the water settle. The grit will fall to the bottom of the bowl. Lift out the clean slices and drain well in a colander.

Roasted Portobello Caps

LARGE PORTOBELLO MUSHROOM CAPS are ideal for roasting because their size prevents them from drying out. Serve the caps just as they are, or use them as a tasty base for grains or vegetables. A roasted portobello cap can even be used as an unconventional "bun" for a burger.

8 to 12 portobello mushrooms

2 to 3 tablespoons extra virgin olive oil

1 garlic clove, minced

2 teaspoons chopped fresh rosemary, thyme, marjoram, oregano, or basil leaves

Salt and freshly ground black pepper

1. Preheat the oven to 500°F. Lightly oil a large shallow roasting or half sheet pan.

2. Carefully remove the stems from the mushrooms. Set aside to use in another recipe or discard. In a small bowl, combine the oil, garlic, and herbs. Brush the caps on both sides with the flavored oil. Place them rounded side up in the pan and sprinkle with salt and pepper to taste.

3. Roast for 6 minutes. Turn and roast for another 5 to 6 minutes, until completely cooked through.

4. Serve hot.

Mixed Roasted Mushrooms in a Soy Vinaigrette

SERVES 4 TO 6

IF THE INCREASING VARIETY of mushrooms at your local produce stand tempts you to expand your repertoire, this is a good recipe to try. I prefer roasting mushrooms over sautéing them for the simple reason that the oven can handle large quantities with ease. If you were to sauté this quantity of mushrooms, you would have to work in batches. With this recipe, you can put the mushrooms in the oven and walk away.

SOY VINAIGRETTE

¼ cup soy sauce

¼ cup rice vinegar

2 tablespoons rice wine or dry sherry

2 garlic cloves, minced

1 scallion, white and tender green parts only, minced

¼ cup toasted sesame oil

MUSHROOMS

2 pounds mixed mushrooms, trimmed and sliced

1 scallion, white and tender green parts only, finely chopped, for garnish

1. Preheat the oven to 450°F. Lightly oil a large shallow roasting or half sheet pan.

2. To make the vinaigrette, combine the soy sauce, vinegar, rice wine, garlic, and scallion in a large bowl. Whisk in the oil until completely emulsified.

3. Add the mushrooms to the vinaigrette and toss to coat. Transfer the mushrooms and marinade to the pan and arrange the mushrooms in a shallow layer.

4. Roast for 20 to 30 minutes, until the mushrooms are browned and tender, stirring or shaking the pan occasionally for even cooking.

5. Transfer the mushrooms to a serving bowl or platter. Serve warm or at room temperature, garnished with the chopped scallion.

Soy-Roasted Shiitakes: **Substitute all fresh shiitake mushrooms (caps only, discard the stems) for the mixed mushrooms to create a dish that complements most Asian menus.**

Roasted Okra

I THINK THIS IS a great way to prepare okra—but you have to like okra. The whole pods emerge from the oven lightly browned, tender, and somewhat sweet. The best way to eat them is with your fingers, biting off and discarding the slightly tougher stem ends.

1 pound okra pods

2 tablespoons extra virgin olive oil

Coarse sea salt or kosher salt

1. Preheat the oven to 450°F. Lightly oil a large shallow roasting or half sheet pan.

2. Combine the okra and oil in a large bowl and toss to coat well. Arrange in a single layer in the pan.

3. Roast for about 15 minutes, until the pods are well browned, shaking the pan occasionally for even cooking.

4. Transfer the okra to a serving bowl. Sprinkle with salt to taste and serve immediately.

Okra Buying Tips Look for green or red pods that are 2 to 3 inches long. Large pods may be tough and stringy, which might be acceptable sliced into a gumbo but definitely are not desirable for roasting whole. The pods are fairly perishable and will keep for only 2 to 3 days in a plastic or paper bag in the refrigerator. Rinse well and pat dry before using.

Oven-Fried Okra

THIS IS VERY SIMILAR to traditional fried okra, with the advantage of no frying and a lot less oil. The crumbs absorb the okra juices, taming the texture and making this an acceptable way to serve a troublesome vegetable—even to those who claim to hate okra.

2 tablespoons canola or peanut oil

1 pound okra pods, trimmed and sliced into ¼-inch-thick rounds

½ cup dry bread crumbs

½ teaspoon salt

½ teaspoon dried thyme

½ teaspoon freshly ground black pepper

1. Preheat the oven to 425°F. Evenly coat a baking sheet with the oil.

2. Combine the okra, bread crumbs, salt, thyme, and pepper in a medium-size bowl. Toss until well coated. Transfer to the baking sheet with a slotted spoon, shaking off excess crumbs.

3. Roast for about 15 minutes, until the pods are well browned and tender, turning once.

4. Serve hot.

Roasted Onion Slices

CRISPY, SWEET ONION RINGS make a delicious topping for sandwiches, meats, and baked or mashed potatoes.

2 large onions, sliced ¼ inch thick
2 tablespoons extra virgin olive oil
Salt and freshly ground black pepper

1. Preheat the oven to 450°F. Lightly oil a large shallow roasting or half sheet pan.

2. Brush the onion slices with the oil and arrange in a single layer in the pan. Sprinkle with salt and pepper to taste.

3. Roast for about 15 minutes. Turn and roast for another 5 to 10 minutes, until the onion slices are tender and well browned.

4. Transfer the slices to a serving bowl or platter. As you move them, the slices will separate into rings. Serve hot.

Caramelized Cipollines

IF YOU ARE GOING to serve roasted onions as a vegetable, it is worth seeking out cipollines during the fall harvest season. Cipollines are very sweet, small, saucer-shaped Italian onions. They are delicious on their own or served as part of an antipasto platter. They also make a superior replacement for creamed onions at Thanksgiving. When peeling these onions, I place them in a bowl and cover them with hot tap water to help loosen the skins.

2 pounds cipollines, peeled

3 tablespoons extra virgin olive oil

2 tablespoons chopped fresh thyme or rosemary leaves (optional)

Salt and freshly ground black pepper

High-quality balsamic vinegar (optional)

1. Preheat the oven to 450°F. Lightly oil a 9 x 13-inch baking dish.

2. In a large bowl, combine the cipollines, oil, and thyme or rosemary, if using. Toss to coat. Arrange in a single layer in the pan.

3. Roast for about 30 minutes, until the onions are well browned and tender, turning once.

4. Transfer the onions to a serving bowl or platter. Season generously with salt and pepper. If desired, drizzle with a little vinegar. Serve hot or warm.

Roasted Parsnip Chips

SERVES 4

THE ONLY PEOPLE I know who like parsnips are gardeners and farmers. That must be because they are the rare individuals who have tasted fresh parsnips, which are quite sweet when roasted. If you need to be converted to the virtues of this unassuming root, grow your own or specifically ask for recently harvested parsnips at a farm stand. Then roast them to bring out their hidden charm.

2 pounds parsnips, peeled and sliced into ½-inch-thick rounds
2 tablespoons extra virgin olive oil
1 tablespoon chopped fresh rosemary leaves
Salt and freshly ground black pepper

1. Preheat the oven to 425°F. Lightly oil a 9 x 13-inch baking dish.

2. In a large bowl, combine the parsnips, oil, rosemary, and salt and pepper to taste. Toss to coat. Arrange in a single layer in the baking dish.

3. Roast for about 30 minutes, until the parsnips are well browned and tender, turning once.

4. Serve hot.

Roasted Peppers

A BOOK ON ROASTING VEGETABLES that does not include roasted peppers would be woefully incomplete. Yet roasting peppers does not require the classic "roasting" technique. Instead, it involves broiling them or charring them over an open flame. No matter—roasted peppers have hundreds of uses, from starring on an antipasto platter or in a pasta sauce to performing a supporting role in salads and casseroles to serving as a minor garnish for all sorts of dishes.

Bell peppers or fresh chile peppers of any color or variety
Extra virgin olive oil (optional)

1. Preheat the broiler. Lightly oil a rimmed baking sheet.

2. Place the peppers on the baking sheet with space between them. Broil 4 inches from the heat for 10 to 20 minutes, until charred all over, turning several times.

3. Place the peppers in a covered bowl, plastic bag, or paper bag. Seal and let steam for about 10 minutes to loosen the skins.

4. Cut slits in the peppers and drain briefly into a small bowl to catch any juices. (The juices may be used with the peppers in a prepared dish, to enhance the peppers' flavor.) Scrape or peel the skins and discard. Discard the seeds and membranes.

5. Leave the peppers whole or slice, as the recipe requires.

6. To store, place in a jar and cover with olive oil. Keep in the refrigerator for up to 2 weeks.

Gas Burner Variation If you have a gas burner and wish to roast one pepper at a time, simply char the pepper over the flame, holding it with tongs. Rotate the pepper so that it chars evenly. This will take about 5 minutes. Proceed as directed above.

Roasted New Potatoes with Garlic and Herbs

THIS IS A RECIPE that is so basic, so perfect, so welcome with any meal that all cooks should have it in their repertoires. New potatoes that show up in farmers' markets and produce stands in the spring and early summer have a delicate nutty, sweet flavor that is worth seeking out. Also worth going out of your way for are fingerling potatoes, so called because of their shape. These potatoes have outstanding fresh flavor—clearly they have not been bred to produce uniform fries for Mickey D's.

2 pounds new or fingerling potatoes, halved

1 head garlic, cloves separated but left unpeeled

1 tablespoon chopped fresh rosemary or thyme leaves

2 tablespoons extra virgin olive oil

Coarse sea salt or kosher salt and freshly ground black pepper

1. Preheat the oven to 425°F. Lightly oil a large shallow roasting or half sheet pan.

2. In a large bowl, combine the potatoes, garlic, and rosemary. Drizzle with the oil and sprinkle lightly with salt and pepper. Toss to coat evenly. Arrange in a single layer in the pan.

3. Roast for 30 to 40 minutes, until the potatoes are tender when pierced with a knife, turning occasionally for even cooking.

4. Transfer the potatoes and garlic to a serving bowl or platter. Sprinkle with additional salt and pepper and serve hot, letting each diner squeeze the roasted garlic out of the skins and over the potatoes while eating.

Roasted Potatoes and Celery Root

SERVES 6

CELERY ROOT, also known as celeriac, is an odd vegetable. This cousin of celery puts all its energy into growing a large knobby tuber rather than stalks. The flavor is remarkably similar to that of the tough outer stalks of celery, but the texture is that of a root vegetable, making it perfect for combining with potatoes. Look for celery root in the market from September through May.

2 pounds small new potatoes, halved
1 celery root (about 1 pound), peeled and cubed
6 shallots, sliced
3 tablespoons extra virgin olive oil
2 teaspoons chopped fresh thyme leaves
Coarse sea salt or kosher salt and freshly ground black pepper

1. Preheat the oven to 425°F. Lightly oil a large shallow roasting or half sheet pan.

2. Combine the potatoes, celery root, and shallots in a large bowl. Sprinkle with the oil and thyme. Toss to coat. Arrange in a single layer in the pan.

3. Roast for about 40 minutes, until the vegetables are lightly browned and tender when pierced with a fork, stirring or shaking the pan occasionally for even cooking.

4. Transfer to a serving bowl or platter. Sprinkle with salt and pepper to taste and serve hot.

Oven-Roasted Fries

SERVES 4

AN EXTREMELY SATISFYING, incredibly easy, low-fat alternative to French fries. Ketchup does just fine as a condiment, but you may want to gild the lily with horseradish-dill sauce.

4 baking potatoes, such as Idaho or russet, skin on, halved lengthwise and cut into thick wedges
2 tablespoons canola oil
2 teaspoons paprika
Salt and freshly ground black pepper
Horseradish-Dill Dipping Sauce (optional; page 46)

1. Preheat the oven to 425°F. Lightly oil a large shallow roasting or half sheet pan.

2. Combine the potatoes, oil, paprika, and salt and pepper to taste in a large bowl. Toss to coat. Arrange cut side down in a single layer in the pan.

3. Roast for about 20 minutes, until the potatoes are well browned and crisp, turning once.

4. Serve hot, with the dipping sauce on the side, if desired.

Horseradish-Dill Dipping Sauce

MAKES 1 CUP

THIS IS A WONDERFUL dipping sauce for roasted potatoes—white or sweet. In truth, it is a good all-purpose dipping sauce, wonderful with all kinds of vegetables and chips.

1 cup sour cream (nonfat works fine)
1 to 2 tablespoons prepared horseradish
2 teaspoons chopped fresh dill
Salt and freshly ground black pepper

1. In a small bowl, combine the sour cream, horseradish, dill, and salt and pepper to taste. Mix well.

2. Let sit for at least 15 minutes to allow the flavor to develop.

3. The sauce is best on the day it is made, but it can be stored in an airtight container in the refrigerator for up to 3 days.

Crispy Smashed Potatoes

LIKE CRISPY POTATO SKINS, only better, because they aren't deep-fried and you don't have to scoop away any potato goodness. These crispy, crunchy potatoes are a favorite with kids. Serve them with ketchup, sour cream and chives, or Horseradish-Dill Dipping Sauce (page 46).

6 baking potatoes, such as Idaho or russet, skin on

2 tablespoons olive or canola oil

Coarse sea salt or kosher salt and freshly ground black pepper

1. Preheat the oven to 400°F.

2. Pierce the potatoes in several places. Roast for about 1 hour, until very tender.

3. Oil a baking sheet. Halve the potatoes lengthwise and arrange them skin side down on the sheet. Using the bottom of a glass, smash each potato to flatten it. Brush the potatoes with the oil and sprinkle with salt and pepper to taste.

4. Roast for 20 minutes. Turn and roast for about another 20 minutes, until the potatoes are browned.

5. Sprinkle with additional salt and serve hot.

Roasted Shallot Confit

THIS RICH, SWEET-AND-SOUR condiment would be a rose by any name, but confit seems as apt an appellation as any. Confit comes from the French for "preserves," and this is a fine way to preserve shallots.

1 pound shallots

9 tablespoons extra virgin olive oil, or more to taste

1 teaspoon chopped fresh rosemary leaves

¼ cup balsamic vinegar, or more to taste

1 tablespoon soy sauce, or more to taste

4 teaspoons water, or more to taste

Salt and freshly ground black pepper

1. Preheat the oven to 425°F. Lightly oil a baking dish large enough to hold the shallots in a single layer.

2. Peel the shallots and cut them into quarters horizontally. Place in the baking dish, toss with 2 tablespoons of the oil, and sprinkle with the rosemary.

3. Roast for about 30 minutes, until the shallots are completely tender and browned, stirring once or twice for even cooking. Let cool slightly.

4. Scrape the shallots into a blender. Add the vinegar, soy sauce, and water and process until fairly smooth. With the motor running, drizzle in the remaining 7 tablespoons oil. Season with salt and pepper to taste. Taste to make sure the balance is right and add more vinegar, soy sauce, water, or oil as needed.

5. Serve at once or store in an airtight jar in the refrigerator for up to 1 week.

The Many Ways to Enjoy Roasted Shallot Confit The shallots and oil contribute a rich, sweet base, balanced by the tart vinegar and salty soy sauce. A tablespoon or two in vegetable soups or baked beans adds a complex flavor. The confit can be served at room temperature and spread on top of roasted, grilled, broiled, or sautéed tofu or mushrooms. It is a wonderful spread for mushroom, fried egg, or turkey sandwiches. It is delicious served as an appetizer spread on French bread. It is even better spread on French bread, topped with a slice of tomato, sprinkled with Parmesan cheese, and run under the broiler until the cheese melts.

Maple-Glazed Rutabagas

SERVES 4

RUTABAGAS ARE ONE of those unfortunate vegetables that suffer a bad reputation because they are often kept until they are old and bitter. Yes, they do store well. But they taste so much better when eaten soon after they are harvested. So if you think you do not like rutabagas, try this recipe in the fall with a freshly harvested root and you may find yourself appreciating this mild-flavored turnip.

2 medium-size rutabagas, peeled and cut into 1-inch cubes
2 tablespoons canola oil
Salt
¼ cup pure maple syrup
2 tablespoons butter, melted
Pinch of nutmeg

1. Preheat the oven to 450°F. Lightly oil a large shallow roasting or half sheet pan.

2. In a large bowl, combine the rutabagas, oil, and salt to taste. Toss to coat. Arrange in a single layer in the pan.

3. Roast for about 25 minutes, until the rutabagas are tender, stirring or shaking the pan occasionally for even cooking.

4. Meanwhile, in a small bowl, combine the maple syrup, butter, and nutmeg. Pour over the rutabagas. Roast for another 10 to 15 minutes, until the rutabagas are well browned and tender.

5. Serve hot.

   Maple-Glazed Turnips: In late spring or early summer, when turnips are freshly harvested, substitute 6 to 8 medium-size turnips for the rutabagas. Reduce the roasting time to 15 minutes in step 3.

Herbed Summer Squash

THE HERB TOPPING adds a savory note without distracting from the essentially delicate flavor of zucchini or yellow summer squash. Choose small, straight squash for the best appearance on the plate.

8 very baby zucchini or yellow summer squash

2 tablespoons extra virgin olive oil, plus more for brushing

Salt and freshly ground black pepper

1 cup lightly packed mixed fresh herb leaves, such as basil, parsley, sage, oregano, rosemary, thyme, and mint

4 garlic cloves, peeled but left whole

1. Preheat the oven to 450°F. Lightly oil a large shallow roasting or half sheet pan.

2. Cut the squash in half lengthwise. Score the flesh in a diamond pattern, cutting almost to the skin. Lightly brush the cut sides with oil and sprinkle generously with salt and pepper.

3. Combine the herbs, garlic, and 2 tablespoons oil in a food processor or blender and process until smooth. Season with salt and pepper to taste. Spread over the cut sides of the squash. Arrange cut side up in the pan.

4. Roast for about 15 minutes, until the squash is tender.

5. Serve hot.

Herbed Pattypan Squash: **These delightful summer squash look like round flying saucers with scalloped edges. Choose squash that are 3 to 4 inches in diameter and cut them in half horizontally. Proceed with the recipe as directed above.**

Zucchini Chips with Feta and Herbs

SERVES 4 TO 6

SALTY, TANGY FETA CHEESE and a handful of fresh herbs give zest to the subtle flavor of zucchini.

2 tablespoons extra virgin olive oil

3 tablespoons freshly squeezed lemon juice

2 pounds small zucchini, sliced into ½-inch-thick rounds

Salt and freshly ground black pepper

2 ounces feta cheese, crumbled (about ½ cup)

¼ cup chopped fresh basil, dill, mint, oregano, sage, or thyme leaves

1. Preheat the oven to 450°F. Generously oil a large shallow roasting or half sheet pan.

2. In a small bowl, whisk together the oil and lemon juice. Arrange the zucchini in a single layer in the pan. Brush with the oil mixture. Sprinkle with salt and pepper to taste.

3. Roast for about 15 minutes, until the zucchini is well browned, turning once.

4. Transfer the zucchini to a serving bowl. Add the cheese and herbs and toss to mix. Taste and add salt and pepper as needed. Serve hot.

Cider-Glazed Acorn Squash

SERVES 4

IN THE CAVITY of each roasted squash half sits a sweetly delicious pool of cider, butter, and maple syrup. As you scrape each forkful of flesh from the skin, dip the fork into the syrup. This is one of the best ways I know to enjoy winter squash.

---

2 medium-size acorn squash, halved and seeded
1½ cups apple cider
3 tablespoons butter
¼ cup pure maple syrup or honey

1. Preheat the oven to 375°F.

2. Place the squash halves cut side down in a baking dish just large enough to hold them. Add about 1 inch of water to the dish.

3. Roast for 30 minutes.

4. Meanwhile, boil the cider in a small saucepan over high heat until it is reduced to about ½ cup. It will become quite thick and syrupy. Stir in the butter and maple syrup until the butter melts.

5. Remove the squash from the baking dish and pour out any water that remains. Arrange the squash cut side up in the dish. Brush the cider sauce over the flesh. Pour the remaining syrup into the cavity of each squash half. If you have any extra syrup, reserve it for the table.

6. Roast for another 15 minutes, until the squash is completely tender.

7. Serve hot, passing any extra syrup at the table.

Honey-Roasted Delicata Squash Rings

SERVES 4

THOSE SLENDER SQUASH cylinders colored yellow, orange, or cream with green streaks are delicata squash. Appropriately named, they have a delicate and sweet flavor. What I like best about them is their shape and tender skins. They can be easily cut into rings and roasted with the skin still on.

1½ to 2 pounds delicata squash
3 tablespoons butter, melted
1 tablespoon honey

1. Preheat the oven to 375°F. Lightly oil a rimmed baking sheet.

2. Slice off the ends of the squash and scoop out the seeds and fibers with a spoon. Cut the squash into 1½-inch-thick rings and place on the baking sheet. Brush the rings on both sides with the butter; you will not use all of it.

3. Roast for 15 minutes.

4. Add the honey to the remaining butter. Turn the squash over, brush with the honey-butter mixture, and roast for another 5 minutes, until tender.

5. Serve hot.

Bejeweled Squash Cubes

SERVES 4 TO 6

A PERFECT WAY to serve squash for Thanksgiving. The squash can be roasted a day ahead if oven space is limited, then reheated in the microwave and combined with the cranberries or cherries, walnuts, and ginger just before serving.

1½ to 2 pounds butternut or other easy-to-peel, smooth-skinned winter squash

3 tablespoons butter, melted

2 tablespoons pure maple syrup

¼ cup dried cranberries or cherries

2 tablespoons red or white wine or water

¼ cup chopped walnuts, toasted (page 211)

2 tablespoons chopped crystallized ginger

1 tablespoon butter (optional)

1. Preheat the oven to 350°F. Lightly oil a large shallow roasting or half sheet pan.

2. Peel the squash; a sharp vegetable peeler will do the job. Cut the squash in half and scoop out the fibers and seeds. Cut the flesh into ½-inch dice. Combine the squash, melted butter, and maple syrup in a large bowl and toss to coat. Arrange in a single layer in the pan.

3. Roast for about 30 minutes, until the squash is tender, stirring every 10 minutes or so for even cooking.

4. Meanwhile, combine the cranberries and wine and heat for 30 seconds in the microwave or in a small saucepan over low heat until soft.

5. When the squash is tender, transfer it to a serving bowl. Add the softened cranberries or cherries, walnuts, and ginger. Toss to mix. If the squash is dry, or if you prefer a richer-tasting dish and don't mind the additional butter, add the 1 tablespoon butter and toss until it is melted. Serve hot.

Spaghetti Squash with Tomato-Garlic Confit

SERVES 4 TO 6

I CONSIDER SPAGHETTI SQUASH a noble vegetable. It has taken the annoying trait of winter squash to be too fibrous and turned it into a virtue. Although spaghetti squash is no substitute for pasta—no matter what the low-carb dieters may say—it does pair well with a sweet-and-sour tomato confit.

---

1 spaghetti squash (3 to 4 pounds)

12 ripe plum tomatoes, halved

1 teaspoon chopped fresh thyme leaves

2 tablespoons extra virgin olive oil

Salt and freshly ground black pepper

8 garlic cloves, sliced

2 teaspoons sherry vinegar, or more to taste

½ teaspoon sugar, or more to taste

2 tablespoons butter

1. Preheat the oven to 375°F.

2. Prick the squash in several places and place on a baking sheet.

3. Roast for about 1¼ hours, until the squash is tender when tested with a fork.

4. Meanwhile, arrange the tomato halves cut side down in a single layer in a lightly oiled 9 x 13-inch baking dish. Scatter the thyme over the tomatoes. Drizzle with the oil and sprinkle with salt and pepper to taste.

5. Roast for 30 minutes. Scatter the garlic slices over the tomatoes. Roast for another 25 to 30 minutes, until the tomatoes are completely tender and beginning to brown.

6. Lift the skins off the tomatoes and discard. Transfer the tomatoes and garlic to a medium-size bowl and mash with the back of a wooden spoon until you have a chunky sauce. Stir in the vinegar and sugar. Taste and adjust the seasonings, adding more vinegar, sugar, salt, or pepper as desired.

7. Cut the roasted squash in half. Discard the seeds and tough fibers. Working over a large bowl and using a fork, scrape out the flesh, which should separate

into individual, spaghetti-like strands. Toss the squash with the butter and season with salt and pepper to taste.

8. To serve, place a mound of squash on each plate and top with a dollop of tomato confit.

Salt and Roasted Vegetables Some people swear by coarse salt and use it all the time when they cook. Others never bother with it; they are happy with the table salt sold in round cylinders at every supermarket. I prefer the very subtle flavor that coarse sea salt adds and use it a lot, especially to finish a dish, but I specify it here only when I think it makes a big difference. For many roasted vegetables, particularly in this chapter, the dishes are simple enough that the choice of salt does matter. So when I specify kosher salt or coarse sea salt, I really do think the recipe turns out better when you use it. When I don't specify, the choice is yours.

Spicy Sweet Potato Wedges

THE ROASTING TEMPERATURE is higher for sweet potatoes than for most other vegetables. Roasting at a lower temperature results in soft—not crispy—potatoes, which is fine for some recipes, but not for these delicious treats.

4 small sweet potatoes

2 tablespoons extra virgin olive oil

½ teaspoon ground cumin

½ teaspoon salt

¼ teaspoon freshly ground black pepper

⅛ teaspoon ground allspice

1. Preheat the oven to 500°F. Lightly oil a large shallow roasting or half sheet pan.

2. Peel the potatoes and cut each lengthwise into 8 wedges. Combine the oil, cumin, salt, pepper, and allspice in a large bowl and mix well. Add the potatoes and toss to coat. Arrange in a single layer in the pan.

3. Place the pan on a rack in the lower third of the oven. Roast for 15 to 20 minutes, until the potatoes are well browned and crisp, turning once.

4. Serve hot.

Garlicky Sweet Potatoes

SERVES 4

WHY ADD SWEET flavors to an already sweet vegetable? Garlic is the perfect foil for this delicious, nutritious vegetable superstar.

3 sweet potatoes, peeled and cut into ½-inch dice
2 tablespoons peanut oil
Salt and freshly ground black pepper
3 tablespoons butter, melted
4 garlic cloves, minced

1. Preheat the oven to 500°F. Lightly oil a large shallow roasting or half sheet pan.

2. In a large bowl, combine the sweet potatoes, oil, and salt and pepper to taste. Toss to coat. Arrange in a single layer in the pan. Do not crowd the potatoes, or the final texture will be too soft and mushy.

3. Place the pan on a rack in the lower third of the oven. Roast for 15 minutes, until the potatoes are tender, stirring or shaking the pan once for even cooking.

4. Combine the butter and garlic in a small bowl. Pour over the potatoes and toss to coat. Roast for another 10 to 15 minutes, until the potatoes are slightly crisp. Do not overcook, or the garlic will become bitter.

5. Serve hot.

Roasted Whole Cherry Tomatoes

SERVES 4 TO 6

A BOWL OF RAW cherry tomatoes on the table is fine, casual dining. Roasting adds a slight smoky aroma and allows the flavor of the herb to soak in. This is a simple and delicious way to prepare cherry tomatoes. Basil is the classic herb to match with tomatoes, but almost any herb from your kitchen garden will complement their flavor.

2 pints cherry tomatoes, stems removed

2 tablespoons extra virgin olive oil

Salt and freshly ground black pepper

1 tablespoon high-quality balsamic vinegar

2 tablespoons chopped fresh basil, tarragon, oregano, thyme, rosemary, sage, or cilantro leaves

1. Preheat the oven to 425°F.

2. In a 9 x 13-inch baking dish, combine the tomatoes and oil and toss to coat. Shake the pan until the tomatoes fall into a single layer.

3. Roast for about 20 minutes, until the tomatoes begin to burst their skins, shaking the pan occasionally for even cooking.

4. Transfer the tomatoes to a serving bowl. Season with salt and pepper to taste. Drizzle the vinegar over the tomatoes and sprinkle with the herbs. Toss gently. Serve warm.

Slow-Roasted Rice-Stuffed Tomatoes

SERVES 4 TO 8

THE SLOW-ROASTING PROCESS does nothing for the appearance of these tomatoes, but, oh, the flavor! The rice slowly absorbs the summery tomato flavor as they roast.

8 medium-size ripe tomatoes

12 large fresh basil leaves

4 garlic cloves, peeled but left whole

½ cup Arborio rice

Salt and freshly ground black pepper

2 tablespoons extra virgin olive oil

1. Preheat the oven to 400°F. Lightly oil an 8-inch baking dish.

2. Remove a ½-inch-thick slice from the stem end of each tomato and reserve. Using a small spoon, carefully scoop the pulp from each tomato into a medium-size bowl; take care to avoid puncturing the walls of the tomato.

3. Arrange the tomatoes hollow side up in the baking dish.

4. Combine the tomato pulp, basil, and garlic in a food processor and process until mostly smooth. Return to the bowl and mix in the rice. Season generously with salt and pepper. Spoon the filling into the tomatoes. Place the reserved slices on top. Drizzle the oil over the tomatoes.

5. Roast for about 50 minutes, until the rice is cooked through and the tomatoes are tender and well browned.

6. Let stand for at least 15 minutes.

7. Serve warm or at room temperature.

Roasted Tomato Sauce

WHEN THE TOMATOES in my garden begin to ripen at a furious pace, I look for quick and easy ways to preserve the excess. This recipe has become one of my favorites in terms of ease of method and usefulness of the final product. The timing of this recipe is based on using a relatively meaty paste tomato. You can use this same method for both cherry tomatoes and juicy beefsteaks, but you may have to adjust the timing. The goal is a thick, not runny, sauce.

6 pounds ripe plum tomatoes, halved and cored

10 to 12 sprigs fresh herbs (optional)

2 or 3 large garlic cloves, sliced (optional)

3 tablespoons extra virgin olive oil

Salt and freshly ground black pepper

1. Preheat the oven to 425°F. Lightly oil a large shallow roasting or half sheet pan.

2. Arrange the tomatoes in a shallow (preferably single) layer in the pan. Strip the leaves from the stems of the herbs, if using, and sprinkle over the tomatoes, along with the garlic, if using. Drizzle the oil over the tomatoes and sprinkle with salt and pepper to taste.

3. Roast for 1¼ to 1½ hours, until the tomatoes have broken down to form a thick sauce and most of the water has evaporated, stirring every 15 minutes to promote even cooking.

4. Let cool slightly and process in a blender or food processor until mostly smooth. Check the seasonings, adding salt and pepper, if desired.

5. Use immediately or store in the refrigerator for up to 4 days or in the freezer for up to 4 months.

A Blank Palette Roasted Tomato Sauce is a wonderfully versatile sauce that can take on different flavors depending on the herbs you use. To make a sauce to serve on pasta, use a blend of basil, thyme, marjoram, and oregano. For a rich enchilada sauce, use a combination of cilantro, oregano, and parsley and add a diced onion and some fresh chiles. Shallots, cumin, cinnamon, and lemon zest will add a Middle Eastern slant. For a neutral sauce that can be seasoned at a later date, skip the herbs entirely. When you are ready to use the sauce, reheat gently and add sautéed mushrooms, onions, shallots, chiles, bell peppers, or garlic and whatever herbs you wish.

Lemon-Garlic Summer Vegetables

SERVES 4 TO 6

THE LEMON-GARLIC MARINADE is baked into the vegetables during the roasting process, brightening the rather bland flavor of summer squash.

2 garlic cloves, peeled but left whole

½ cup lightly packed mixed fresh herb leaves, such as basil, mint, parsley, chives, sage, and thyme

Zest and juice of 1 small lemon

3 tablespoons extra virgin olive oil

Salt and freshly ground black pepper

2 small yellow summer squash, cut into matchsticks

2 small zucchini, cut into matchsticks

1 red bell pepper, cut into matchsticks

1 yellow bell pepper, cut into matchsticks

1 carrot, cut into matchsticks

1. Preheat the oven to 425°F. Lightly oil a large shallow roasting or half sheet pan.

2. In a food processor, combine the garlic, herbs, and lemon zest and finely mince. Add the lemon juice and process until smooth. With the motor running, slowly add the oil and process until it is fully incorporated. Season with salt and pepper to taste.

3. In a large bowl, combine the summer squash, zucchini, bell peppers, and carrot. Pour the lemon-herb mixture over the vegetables and toss to coat. Arrange in a single layer in the pan.

4. Roast for 15 to 20 minutes, until the vegetables are lightly browned and tender, stirring or shaking the pan occasionally for even cooking.

5. Transfer the vegetables to a serving bowl or platter. Season with more salt and pepper, if needed. Serve warm or at room temperature.

Summer Vegetable Gratin

BUTTERY CRUMBS ENHANCE the flavor of the sweet vegetables, while mixing in the fresh basil adds a definite summery touch. This is a delicious way to prepare vegetables, which can be varied depending on what you have on hand.

---

6 cups diced mixed summer vegetables, such as bell peppers, leeks, carrots, corn, zucchini, yellow summer squash, green beans, wax beans, and broccoli (include at least 4 different vegetables in the mix)

4 to 8 garlic cloves (optional), thinly sliced

2 tablespoons extra virgin olive oil

Salt and freshly ground black pepper

2 tablespoons butter

½ cup dry bread crumbs

2 tablespoons chopped fresh basil leaves

1. Preheat the oven to 425°F. Lightly oil a large shallow roasting or half sheet pan.

2. In a large bowl, combine the vegetables and garlic, if using. Add the oil and salt and pepper to taste. Toss to coat. Arrange in a single layer in the pan.

3. Roast for 25 to 30 minutes, until the vegetables are tender and lightly browned, stirring or shaking the pan occasionally for even cooking.

4. Meanwhile, melt the butter in a large skillet over medium heat. Add the bread crumbs and sauté until lightly toasted, about 5 minutes.

5. When the vegetables are tender, transfer them to a shallow serving bowl. Mix in the basil. Top with the bread crumbs and serve at once.

Herb-Roasted Root Vegetables

SERVES 4 TO 6

HERE'S YOUR BASIC vegetable feast—perfect for a holiday meal. The vegetables hold up well on a buffet table or in a covered dish if you cannot serve them immediately. Be forewarned, however, that what starts out looking like a huge amount of food reduces down to a fairly small serving size. The roasting time is longer for this large quantity than it would be for a smaller amount.

3 to 4 pounds mixed root vegetables, such as beets, carrots, kohlrabi, parsnips, rutabagas, sweet potatoes, turnips, and white potatoes, peeled and cut into 1-inch cubes

1 cup pearl onions or shallots, peeled but left whole (cut shallots in half or into quarters if large)

1 head garlic, cloves separated and peeled

3 tablespoons extra virgin olive oil

2 tablespoons chopped fresh rosemary, thyme, or sage leaves

Coarse sea salt or kosher salt and freshly ground black pepper

1 tablespoon chopped fresh parsley leaves, for garnish

1. Preheat the oven to 425°F. Lightly oil a large shallow roasting or half sheet pan.

2. In a large bowl, combine the vegetables, pearl onions, and garlic. Add the oil, herbs, and salt and pepper to taste. Toss to coat. Arrange in a shallow (preferably single) layer in the pan.

3. Roast for about 1 hour, until the vegetables are lightly browned and tender, stirring or shaking the pan occasionally for even cooking.

4. Transfer the vegetables to a serving platter, taste, and add more salt and pepper, if needed. Sprinkle with the parsley and serve.

SNACKS, STARTERS, AND SOUPS

Crunchy Chickpea Snacks

Tomato-Parmesan Bruschetta

Antipasto of Roasted Vegetables

Sweet-and-Sour Cipollines

Indian Summer Pepper Relish

Roasted Corn Salsa

Salsa Verde

Middle Eastern Eggplant Spread

Baba Ghanoush

Ten Mothers Garlic Soup

Roasted Squash and Apple Bisque

Curried Roasted Squash Soup

Tortellini in Roasted Tomato Broth

Roasted Vegetable Stock

Crunchy Chickpea Snacks

A DELICIOUS ALTERNATIVE to roasted nuts, these crunchy chickpeas are similar to the roasted chickpeas sold by street vendors throughout the Middle East. Double roasting is necessary to develop a crispy texture. A few chickpeas may explode in the oven during roasting, so be prepared for a little cleanup afterward. But these easy-to-make nuggets are worth it. Serve as a snack with drinks, or toss on top of a green salad.

Two 15.5-ounce cans chickpeas or 3 cups cooked chickpeas, rinsed and drained

3 tablespoons extra virgin olive oil

1 teaspoon granulated onion powder

1 teaspoon granulated garlic powder

½ teaspoon ground cumin

½ teaspoon cayenne pepper

Coarse sea salt or kosher salt

1. Preheat the oven to 350°F. Lightly oil a rimmed baking sheet.

2. Spread out the chickpeas in a single layer on the baking sheet.

3. Roast for about 20 minutes, until the chickpeas are dry to the touch. Remove from the oven and increase the temperature to 425°F.

4. Drizzle the oil over the chickpeas. Sprinkle with the onion powder, garlic powder, cumin, and cayenne. Shake the pan to coat.

5. Roast for 15 to 20 minutes, until the chickpeas are crispy and lightly browned.

6. Sprinkle the chickpeas lightly with salt. Let cool completely.

7. Store in an airtight container for up to 1 month.

Cooking Chickpeas Chickpeas are one of my favorite beans to eat, but I use canned chickpeas more often than dried for the simple reason that they can take a long time to cook. To cook chickpeas, soak them overnight in water that covers them by at least 2 inches. In the morning, drain and transfer to a large saucepan. Add fresh water to cover by at least 2 inches. Season with salt and cumin, if desired. Bring to a boil, skimming off any foam that rises to the top. Reduce the heat to maintain a slow boil, place the lid on the pot so it is slightly askew, and boil gently until the chickpeas are tender. This can take 2 to 2½ hours, depending on the age of the beans. Taste several chickpeas to be sure they are completely done before removing them from the heat. Chickpeas are an especially good candidate for a pressure cooker. Follow the manufacturer's directions regarding cooking times and amounts.

Tomato-Parmesan Bruschetta

SERVES 5 TO 10

THESE LITTLE TOASTS make a fine hors d'oeuvre, a delicious snack, and a perfect accompaniment to soup or salad.

1 pound ripe plum tomatoes, halved and cored

½ pound mushrooms, trimmed and sliced

6 garlic cloves, peeled but left whole

1 tablespoon chopped fresh rosemary leaves

Salt and freshly ground black pepper

4 tablespoons extra virgin olive oil

10 slices French bread, lightly toasted

Freshly shaved Parmesan cheese

1. Preheat the oven to 450°F. Lightly oil a 9 x 13-inch baking dish.

2. Place the tomatoes cut side down in the baking dish. Scatter the mushrooms and garlic in the dish. Sprinkle the rosemary and salt and pepper to taste over the vegetables. Pour 3 tablespoons of the oil over all.

3. Roast for about 30 minutes, until the mushrooms are browned and the tomatoes are soft, stirring occasionally for even cooking. Remove from the oven and preheat the broiler.

4. Lift the skins off the tomatoes and discard. Scrape the vegetables into a bowl and mash with a fork. Brush the bread slices with the remaining 1 tablespoon oil. Spread the tomato mixture on the bread and top each slice with a shaving of Parmesan. Arrange on a baking sheet.

5. Broil for about 2 minutes, until the cheese is melted and bubbly.

6. Serve at once.

Roasted Vegetable Bruschetta Roasted vegetables make a fine topping for bruschetta. Begin with lightly toasted bread. Drizzle high-quality olive oil over the bread. If your topping doesn't contain garlic, rub each slice with a cut garlic clove. Here are some different topping combinations to consider.

- Top each slice with some Garlic Puree (page 28) and a shaving of Parmesan cheese.
- Top each slice with roasted mushrooms and a shaving of Parmesan cheese, grated Gruyère cheese, or crumbled feta cheese.
- Spread each slice with mild, fresh goat cheese, such as Montrachet, and top with roasted mixed root vegetables.
- Spread each slice with Roasted Tomato Sauce (page 62), then sprinkle with chopped fresh herbs and grated Parmesan cheese or crumbled feta cheese.
- Spread each slice with Indian Summer Pepper Relish (page 75).
- Top each bread slice with a slice of roasted zucchini and a crumble of feta cheese.
- Top each slice with a spoonful of Roasted Shallot Confit (page 48) and a shaving of Parmesan cheese.

Parmesan Cheese: Buy the Real Stuff When you go to buy Parmesan cheese, look for the real stuff: Parmigiano-Reggiano. This is an all-natural cheese made in the area around Parma, Italy. It has a sweet, salty, nutty flavor with a slightly granular texture. You'll pay more for this cheese, but it is usually worth the price. Although purchased grated cheese (never a good idea) is often finely grated, I prefer to use the large holes of my box grater to get bigger, more flavorful pieces of cheese. If you are using Parmigiano-Reggiano to garnish a salad or to top bruschetta, you may want to shave the cheese to get even larger pieces. Use a vegetable peeler and strip off very thin slices.

Antipasto of Roasted Vegetables

SERVES 4 TO 6

THIS ANTIPASTO CAN BE a meal in itself with a few additions, such as sliced fresh mozzarella cheese. As an antipasto, it is nicely followed by a pasta simply dressed with fresh tomato sauce or perhaps roasted peppers and shaved Parmesan cheese. In any case, serve these delicious roasted vegetables with fresh Italian bread and an Italian white wine, such as soave or pinot grigio.

1 large eggplant, peeled and sliced into ⅜-inch-thick rounds

Extra virgin olive oil

Salt and freshly ground black pepper

2 small to medium-size zucchini, cut into 3-inch-long spears

½ pound green beans or asparagus, ends or bottoms trimmed

2 tablespoons red wine vinegar

2 garlic cloves, minced

1½ teaspoons anchovy paste, or salt to taste

1 tablespoon chopped fresh mint, thyme, oregano, or basil leaves

2 tablespoons extra virgin olive oil

1 roasted yellow bell pepper (page 42), cut into strips

1 roasted red bell pepper (page 42), cut into strips

½ cup brine-cured black olives, such as Kalamata

1 tablespoon capers, drained

1. Preheat the oven to 450°F. Lightly oil two rimmed baking sheets.

2. To make the vegetables, brush the eggplant slices with oil, season with salt and pepper to taste, and arrange in a single layer on one of the baking sheets. Brush the zucchini spears with oil and place flesh side down on one half of the second baking sheet. Arrange the green beans on the other half of the baking sheet. Drizzle a little oil over the beans and spread with a brush.

3. Place the baking sheets side by side in the oven. Roast for 20 to 25 minutes, until the vegetables are tender, turning the eggplant and zucchini once and rolling the green beans for even cooking. (If the baking sheets do not fit side by side, place one on the middle rack and the other on the bottom rack and rotate the sheets halfway through the roasting process.)

4. Meanwhile, prepare the marinade. Combine the vinegar, garlic, anchovy paste or salt, and herbs in a small bowl. Whisk in the oil until fully emulsified.

5. Arrange the roasted eggplant, zucchini, green beans, and peppers on a large serving platter. Add the olives. Pour the marinade over all. Scatter the capers on top.

6. Set aside to marinate for at least 30 minutes.

7. Serve at room temperature.

Sweet-and-Sour Cipollines

CIPOLLINES ARE SMALL, sweet onions. Look for them in the market from September through February. Roasted and marinated in vinegar, they make an excellent addition to an antipasto platter.

2 pounds cipollines, peeled

3 tablespoons extra virgin olive oil

2 tablespoons chopped fresh rosemary leaves

Salt and freshly ground black pepper

3 tablespoons red wine vinegar

Pinch of nutmeg

1. Preheat the oven to 450°F. Lightly oil a 9 x 13-inch baking dish.

2. In a large bowl, combine the cipollines, oil, and rosemary. Season generously with salt and pepper and toss to coat. Arrange in a single layer in the dish.

3. Roast for about 30 minutes, until the onions are well browned and tender, turning once.

4. Transfer the onions to a shallow bowl. Drizzle the vinegar over the onions and sprinkle with the nutmeg. Taste and adjust the seasonings as needed. Let stand for at least 1 hour at room temperature, stirring occasionally. Or place in an airtight container and refrigerate for up to 1 week. Invert occasionally to remoisten the onions with the vinegar.

5. Serve at room temperature.

Indian Summer Pepper Relish

HOW DO I love this? Let me count the ways. It is the perfect addition to a cheese-and-cracker board. It is terrific on a grilled cheddar sandwich on whole wheat and wonderful with goat cheese on French bread. It completes a veggie burger, makes a fine dip for raw veggies or corn chips, and can serve as a topping for simply cooked fish or chicken.

2 red bell peppers

1 ear corn

2 scallions, white and tender green parts only, finely chopped

1 tablespoon chopped fresh basil leaves

1 tablespoon extra virgin olive oil

1 tablespoon red wine vinegar

Salt and freshly ground black pepper

1 to 3 teaspoons sugar (optional)

1. Preheat the broiler. Lightly oil a rimmed baking sheet.

2. Place the bell peppers and corn on the baking sheet with space between them. Broil 4 inches from the heat for 10 to 20 minutes, until charred all over, turning several times.

3. Place the peppers in a covered bowl, plastic bag, or paper bag. Seal and let steam for about 10 minutes to loosen the skins. Strip the corn kernels from the cob and place in a medium-size bowl.

4. Cut slits in the peppers and drain briefly into the bowl with the corn to catch any juices. Scrape or peel off the skins and discard. Discard the seeds and membranes. Finely chop the peppers and add to the corn, along with the scallions, basil, oil, and vinegar. Mix well. Season with salt and pepper to taste. Add the sugar to balance the flavors, if needed.

5. Let stand for at least 15 minutes to allow the flavors to blend.

6. Serve at room temperature.

Roasted Corn Salsa

SWEET, HOT, AND FRUITY are the impressions this salsa leaves. It is great for chips and works well as a topping for broiled fish or chicken.

Kernels from 2 ears corn

1 medium-size jalapeño, thinly sliced (seeding is optional)

1 small green bell pepper, diced

3 garlic cloves, thinly sliced

1 tablespoon extra virgin olive oil

Salt and freshly ground black pepper

1 large ripe beefsteak or 3 small ripe plum tomatoes, seeded and finely chopped

2 tablespoons freshly squeezed lime juice

1 tablespoon chopped fresh cilantro leaves

1 scallion, white and tender green parts only, chopped

1. Preheat the oven to 425°F. Lightly oil a large shallow roasting or half sheet pan.

2. In a large bowl, combine the corn, jalapeño, bell pepper, and garlic. Add the oil and toss to coat. Season with salt and pepper to taste. Arrange in a single layer in the pan. Do not wash the bowl.

3. Roast for 20 to 30 minutes, until the vegetables are tender and lightly browned, stirring occasionally.

4. Return the roasted vegetables to the bowl and combine with the tomatoes, lime juice, cilantro, and scallion. Taste and adjust the seasonings as needed. You may want to add more salt to balance the sweetness of the corn.

5. Let stand, covered, for at least 1 hour to allow the flavors to develop. Taste and adjust the seasonings, if needed.

6. Serve at once, or cover and refrigerate. The salsa will keep for up to 4 days, but it is best on the day it is made. Serve at room temperature.

Salsa Verde

TOMATILLOS ARE THE quintessential Mexican "tomatoes," although they are not really tomatoes at all. Fresh tomatillos show up in markets when red tomatoes do. These green fruits are covered with a papery husk that must be peeled away. Raw, they are quite tart. But roasting brings out lemony, herbal flavors, which become almost floral when combined with lime and cilantro. This salsa is delicious with chips or spooned onto any dish where a tomato-based salsa would work.

2 pints tomatillos (about 1 pound)
2 jalapeños, seeded and chopped
½ small onion, chopped
2 tablespoons extra virgin olive oil
2 tablespoons chopped fresh cilantro leaves, or to taste
2 teaspoons freshly squeezed lime juice, or to taste
Salt and freshly ground black pepper

1. Preheat the oven to 425°F. Lightly oil a rimmed baking sheet or small roasting pan.

2. Peel the dry, papery skin from the tomatillos, rinse, and pat dry. Cut the tomatillos into quarters and place in a medium-size bowl with the jalapeños and onion. Add the oil and toss to coat. Arrange in a single layer on the baking sheet.

3. Roast for about 15 minutes, until the tomatillos are quite soft.

4. Combine the roasted vegetables and cilantro in a food processor and pulse to make a rough puree.

5. Pour into a small bowl and add the lime juice and salt and pepper to taste. Let stand for at least 15 minutes to allow the flavors to blend. Taste and adjust the seasonings, adding more cilantro, lime juice, salt, or pepper as needed.

6. This salsa is best on the day it is made, but it can be stored in the refrigerator, tightly covered, for up to 3 days. Serve at room temperature.

Middle Eastern Eggplant Spread

THE COMBINATION OF roasted eggplant and caramelized onions makes this a very hearty—almost meatlike—spread. It makes a delicious sandwich with sliced tomatoes and tzatziki (page 146) in a pita, but my preference is to serve it with crackers or flatbread as an appetizer.

2 pounds eggplant (1 large)

2 medium-size onions, thinly sliced

2 tablespoons extra virgin olive oil

3 tablespoons freshly squeezed lemon juice, or more to taste

¼ cup lightly packed finely chopped fresh parsley leaves

¼ cup finely chopped fresh chives or scallions, white and tender green parts only

2 tablespoons finely chopped fresh cilantro leaves

Salt and freshly ground black pepper

Flatbread or sesame crackers (optional)

1. Preheat the oven to 400°F.

2. Prick the eggplant with a fork in several places on all sides. Place on a baking sheet. Combine the onions and oil on another baking sheet and toss to coat. Arrange in a single layer.

3. Place the baking sheets side by side in the oven. Roast the onions for 20 to 25 minutes, until well browned and tender. Roast the eggplant for 40 to 60 minutes, until completely soft and collapsed, turning occasionally for even cooking. (If the baking sheets do not fit side by side, place one on the middle rack and the other on the bottom rack and rotate the sheets once or twice during the roasting process.)

4. Place the eggplant in a colander, slice open with a knife, and let drain and cool for about 30 minutes.

5. Scrape the eggplant flesh onto a cutting board and discard the skin. Scrape the onions onto the cutting board on top of the eggplant. Finely chop everything until you have a paste.

6. In a medium-size bowl, combine the eggplant-onion mixture, lemon juice, parsley, chives, and cilantro. Mix well. Season with salt and pepper to taste.

Taste and adjust the seasonings, adding more salt, pepper, and lemon juice as needed.

7. Cover and let stand for at least 30 minutes to allow the flavors to blend.

8. Serve at room temperature with flatbread or sesame crackers for scooping up the dip, if desired.

Baba Ghanoush

THERE ARE TWO KEY STEPS in this recipe: piercing the eggplant before roasting and draining it after roasting. Piercing is essential because the eggplant *really* will explode in your oven if you do not (and it is not easy to clean up). Draining is essential because it removes any bitter juices and greatly improves the flavor of this classic Middle Eastern dip.

---

2 pounds eggplant (1 large)

¼ cup lightly packed fresh flat-leaf parsley leaves

2 garlic cloves, peeled but left whole

3 tablespoons freshly squeezed lemon juice, or more to taste

2 tablespoons tahini (sesame paste)

2 tablespoons extra virgin olive oil

1 teaspoon salt, or more to taste

Freshly ground black pepper

Flatbread or sesame crackers (optional)

1. Preheat the oven to 400°F.

2. Prick the eggplant with a fork in several places on all sides. Place on a baking sheet.

3. Roast for 40 to 60 minutes, until the eggplant is completely soft and collapsed, turning it occasionally.

4. Place the eggplant in a colander, slice open with a knife, and let drain and cool for about 30 minutes.

5. Combine the parsley and garlic in a food processor and process until finely chopped. Remove the eggplant flesh from the skin and add the flesh to the food processor, along with the lemon juice, tahini, oil, salt, and pepper to taste. Process until fairly smooth. Taste and adjust the seasonings, adding more salt, pepper, or lemon juice as needed.

6. Cover and let stand for at least 30 minutes to allow the flavors to blend.

7. Serve at room temperature with flatbread or sesame crackers for scooping up the dip, if desired.

Ten Mothers Garlic Soup

THERE IS AN OLD folk saying that garlic is as good as ten mothers. It must be true when it comes to this soup—a comforting broth redolent with garlic and enriched with the vitamins and minerals of fresh spinach.

2 heads garlic

2 teaspoons extra virgin olive oil

5 cups high-quality neutral-tasting chicken or vegetable broth

4 cups chopped fresh spinach leaves, tough stems discarded

1. Preheat the oven to 425°F.

2. Remove the outer papery covering of the garlic. Slice off the top of each head so most of the cloves are exposed. Place on a square of aluminum foil for easy cleanup, or select the smallest baking dish you have. Drizzle 1 teaspoon oil over each head. Fold the foil over the garlic to completely enclose it, or cover the baking dish with foil.

3. Roast for about 45 minutes, until the garlic is completely soft and lightly browned.

4. When cool enough to handle, squeeze the garlic pulp into a medium-size saucepan. Add the broth and stir well to combine. Simmer for 15 minutes to allow the flavors to blend.

5. Just before serving, stir in the spinach and simmer until wilted, about 4 minutes. Stir vigorously (the garlic has a tendency to settle out).

6. Serve hot.

Note: **If you have some Garlic Puree (page 28) on hand, you can substitute 2 tablespoons of it for the 2 garlic heads and 2 teaspoons oil.**

Roasted Squash and Apple Bisque

SERVES 4 TO 6

ROASTING THE SQUASH with the apples and cider gives the soup a very strong apple presence, which is balanced by the earthy flavors of leek and garlic. This harvest soup is a wonderful celebration of fall, perfect to start a Thanksgiving feast or provide a warm-up after a day of hiking or picking apples.

3 pounds butternut squash, peeled, seeded, and cut into 2-inch cubes

2 tart apples, such as Granny Smith, peeled, cored, and chopped

1 leek, white part only, sliced

4 garlic cloves, peeled but left whole

¼ cup (½ stick) butter, cut into pieces

2 cups apple cider

3 cups high-quality neutral-tasting chicken or vegetable broth

Salt and freshly ground black pepper

Chopped crystallized ginger or ground nutmeg, for garnish

1. Preheat the oven to 425°F. Lightly oil a 9 x 13-inch baking dish.

2. Combine the squash, apples, leek, and garlic in the baking dish. Dot with the butter. Pour ½ cup of the cider into the dish and cover with aluminum foil.

3. Roast for 30 minutes. Remove the foil, then roast for another 30 minutes, until the squash is completely soft.

4. Divide the vegetables into 3 batches and puree in a blender or food processor, adding the remaining 1½ cups cider and some of the broth to each batch. Combine the batches in a large saucepan, adding any remaining broth. Bring to a simmer. Season with salt and pepper to taste.

5. Serve hot, topping each bowl with a few pieces of crystallized ginger or a sprinkle of nutmeg.

Curried Roasted Squash Soup

SERVES 6

THE POWERFUL FRAGRANCE of curry plays nicely off the sweet squash, while the coconut milk and lime juice counteract the heat.

---

1 medium-size to large butternut squash (3 to 4 pounds), halved and seeded

2 tablespoons peanut or canola oil

1 tablespoon curry powder

1 tablespoon peeled and minced fresh ginger

1 teaspoon cumin seeds

½ teaspoon red pepper flakes

4 garlic cloves, minced

1½ cups high-quality neutral-tasting chicken or vegetable broth

1½ cups unsweetened coconut milk

Juice of 1 lime (about 2 tablespoons), or to taste

Salt and freshly ground black pepper

¼ cup chopped fresh cilantro leaves

1. Preheat the oven to 400°F.

2. Place the squash flesh side down in a 9 x 13-inch baking dish. Roast for about 1 hour, until the squash is completely tender. Let cool slightly.

3. Meanwhile, heat the oil in a small skillet over medium-low heat. Add the curry, ginger, cumin seeds, and red pepper flakes. Simmer until fragrant, about 3 minutes. Add the garlic and simmer for about 2 minutes more, until the garlic just begins to color. Remove from the heat.

4. Scoop the flesh from the squash. Combine half the squash in a blender with half the spices and half the broth. Process until smooth. Transfer to a large saucepan. Repeat with the remaining squash, spices, and broth. Add the coconut milk, lime juice, and salt and pepper to taste to the soup. Taste and adjust the seasonings, adding more salt, pepper, or lime juice as needed.

5. Reheat over medium heat until hot, stirring frequently. Just before serving, stir in the cilantro.

6. Serve hot.

Tortellini in Roasted Tomato Broth

SERVES 4 TO 6

THE COMBINATION OF roasted tomatoes and vegetable broth provides a rich, flavorful base for this very simple soup. If you are using a commercial vegetable broth, taste and make sure you like its flavor before adding it to the tomatoes. Some commercial brands have very strong—even unpleasant—flavors. They can ruin your soup!

4 pounds ripe plum tomatoes, halved and cored

6 large garlic cloves, peeled but left whole

4 tablespoons extra virgin olive oil

Salt and freshly ground black pepper

1 fennel bulb, cut into matchsticks, stalks discarded, and a few feathery leaves chopped for garnish

1 pound fresh or frozen tortellini

4 cups high-quality neutral-tasting chicken or vegetable broth

1. Preheat the oven to 425°F. Lightly oil a large shallow roasting pan or half sheet pan and a 9 x 13-inch baking dish.

2. Arrange the tomatoes cut side up in a shallow (preferably single) layer in the pan. Sprinkle the garlic over the tomatoes. Drizzle 3 tablespoons of the oil over the tomatoes and sprinkle generously with salt and pepper.

3. In the baking dish, toss the fennel with the remaining 1 tablespoon oil and arrange in a single layer.

4. Place the pan and baking dish side by side in the oven. (If they do not fit side by side, place the tomatoes on the lower rack.) Roast the fennel for 10 to 15 minutes, until tender and lightly browned. Remove from the oven and set aside. Roast the tomatoes for 1 to 1¼ hours, until they are completely soft and have given up a lot of juice, stirring every 15 minutes. Let cool slightly.

5. Meanwhile, cook the tortellini in a large pot of salted boiling water until al dente. Drain.

6. Pass the tomatoes and garlic through a food mill to remove the tomato seeds and skins and puree the garlic. Transfer to a large saucepan and add the broth.

Bring to a simmer over medium heat. Add the tortellini and fennel and simmer for 5 minutes to heat through. Season with salt and pepper to taste.

7. Serve hot, garnished with the chopped fennel leaves.

Much Depends on Broth A good soup depends on a good broth. Although there are several commercial soup companies that make good chicken broths, good taste seems to fly out the window when it comes to vegetable broths. Most taste unpleasantly vegetal; some have dominant mushroom or tomato flavors. The only canned vegetable broth I've found that I like for cooking (but not for serving plain) is Westbrae's Un-Chicken Broth.

Roasted Vegetable Stock

THIS STOCK CAN BE USED as the foundation of a soup. It is a little on the sweet side because the vegetables are roasted. To reduce the sweetness, substitute celery or celery root for the carrots.

4 carrots, sliced

4 celery ribs, sliced

1 leek, white and light green parts only, sliced

1 onion, sliced

6 garlic cloves, peeled but left whole

2 tablespoons peanut or canola oil

1 cup boiling water

7 cups water

1 teaspoon soy sauce, or more to taste

½ teaspoon black peppercorns

12 sprigs fresh parsley

1 bay leaf

2 sprigs fresh thyme or sage

Salt

1. Preheat the oven to 425°F.

2. Combine the carrots, celery, leek, onion, and garlic in a large shallow roasting pan. Add the oil and toss to coat. Arrange in a single layer.

3. Roast for about 40 minutes, until the vegetables are well browned.

4. Transfer the vegetables to a soup pot. Pour the 1 cup boiling water into the roasting pan and stir to scrape up the browned bits clinging to the pan. Scrape into the soup pot. Add the 7 cups water, soy sauce, peppercorns, parsley, bay leaf, and thyme. Bring to a boil. Cover, reduce the heat, and simmer for 30 minutes.

5. Strain the stock through a fine metal sieve, pressing with a spoon to extract as much liquid as possible. Taste and add salt or more soy sauce.

6. Use at once or store in an airtight container in the refrigerator for up to 5 days or in the freezer for up to 6 months.

SUMPTUOUS SALADS

Mixed Greens with Roasted Vegetables

Asparagus Vinaigrette

Roasted Asparagus and Potato Salad

Roasted Beet and Potato Salad

Blue Cheese, Roasted Beet, and Endive Salad

Russian Winter Vegetable Salad

Green Bean and Carrot Vinaigrette

Frisée Salad with Warm Lentils, Goat Cheese, and Roasted Onions

Marinated Roasted Pepper and Olive Salad

Roasted Potato Salad with Herbs and Parmesan Dressing

Roasted Potato and Green Bean Salad

Summer Pasta Salad with Roasted Vegetables

Pesto Pasta Salad with Roasted Vegetables

Pasta Salad with Roasted Vegetables and Olive Vinaigrette

Cold Sesame Noodles with Soy-Roasted Shiitakes

Cranberry-Nut Wild Rice Salad

Mixed Greens with Roasted Vegetables

SERVES 6 TO 8

A FEAST OF VEGETABLES! This is a great salad to serve when you want to introduce a nonbeliever to the intense flavors of roasted vegetables. The sweetly caramelized vegetables are a perfect match for the lightly dressed greens. This makes a fine main course salad with a loaf of fresh bread and, perhaps, a selection of cheese.

1 pound new potatoes, preferably red or blue fingerlings, cut into wedges

1 pound beets, peeled and cut into matchsticks

½ pound baby carrots

½ pound green beans, ends trimmed

1 red bell pepper, cut into matchsticks

1 small onion, halved and slivered

1 head garlic, cloves separated and peeled

4 tablespoons extra virgin olive oil

Coarse sea salt or kosher salt and freshly ground black pepper

12 cups torn mixed salad greens or mesclun, including some bitter or strong-tasting greens such as arugula, radicchio, or frisée

2 teaspoons sherry, balsamic, or red wine vinegar

1. Preheat the oven to 450°F. Lightly oil a large shallow roasting or half sheet pan.

2. In a large bowl, combine the potatoes, beets, carrots, green beans, red pepper, onion, and garlic. Add 3 tablespoons of the oil and toss well. Season with salt and pepper to taste. Arrange in a shallow (preferably single) layer in the pan.

3. Roast for 30 to 40 minutes, until the vegetables are tender and well browned, stirring or shaking the pan occasionally for even cooking. Let cool to room temperature. This can be done several hours in advance.

4. Just before serving, in a large salad bowl, toss the salad greens with the remaining 1 tablespoon oil and the vinegar. Add the vegetables and toss again. Serve at once.

Asparagus Vinaigrette

SERVES 4

ASPARAGUS IS NOTHING LESS than a celebration of spring. It is with deep regret that I note supermarkets are stocking it year-round these days. Do yourself a favor and save your appetite for the fresh, locally harvested spears. Then enjoy the nutty, sweet flavors of this simple salad.

1 large garlic clove, minced

2 tablespoons sherry vinegar or red wine vinegar

½ teaspoon Dijon mustard

6 tablespoons extra virgin olive oil

Salt and freshly ground black pepper

1 pound asparagus (12 to 16 medium-thick spears), bottoms trimmed

1. Preheat the oven to 400°F. Lightly oil a rimmed baking sheet or 9 x 13-inch baking dish.

2. In a small bowl, combine the garlic, vinegar, and mustard. Whisk in the oil until it is completely emulsified. Season with salt and pepper to taste.

3. Arrange the asparagus in a single layer on the baking sheet or in the baking dish. Drizzle 2 tablespoons of the vinaigrette over the asparagus and roll until well coated.

4. Roast for about 15 minutes, until the asparagus is tender and lightly browned, shaking the pan a few times for even browning.

5. Transfer the asparagus to a serving platter and pour on the remaining vinaigrette. Serve warm or at room temperature.

Buying and Storing Asparagus You'll find bunches of asparagus standing upright in the produce section of the supermarket. Select a bunch of similar-size spears, choosing thicker rather than thinner stems. Make sure the tips are all intact. Turn the bunch over and be sure the woody ends are not completely dried out. When you get the asparagus home, remove the rubber bands or ties that bind the spears and store them in a plastic bag in the refrigerator for up to 3 days.

Roasted Asparagus and Potato Salad

SERVES 4

A DELECTABLE COMBINATION of flavors and textures. The crisp, bitter greens provide a lively background for the tender, sweet asparagus and the crunchy, earthy potatoes.

4 baking potatoes, such as Idaho or russet, skin on

6 tablespoons extra virgin olive oil

Salt and freshly ground black pepper

2 tablespoons red wine vinegar

¼ teaspoon Dijon mustard

1 garlic clove, minced

1 pound asparagus (12 to 16 medium-thick spears), bottoms trimmed and cut into 2-inch pieces

12 cups torn mixed salad greens or mesclun, including some bitter or strong-tasting greens such as arugula, watercress, or endive

1 cup small cherry tomatoes, for garnish

1. Preheat the oven to 425°F.

2. Cut the potatoes in half lengthwise. Cut each half into 6 to 8 thin wedges. Place in a large bowl. Add 2 tablespoons of the oil and salt and pepper to taste. Toss to coat. Arrange in a single layer on a rimmed baking sheet. Do not wash the bowl.

3. In a small bowl, combine the vinegar, mustard, and garlic. Whisk in the remaining 4 tablespoons oil until fully emulsified. Add salt and pepper to taste.

4. Place the asparagus in the bowl that held the potatoes. Add about half the dressing and toss to coat. Arrange in a single layer on another rimmed baking sheet. Do not wash the bowl.

5. Place the baking sheets side by side in the oven. Roast the asparagus for about 20 minutes, until tender and lightly browned, shaking the pan a few times for even browning. Roast the potatoes for about 25 minutes, until tender and well browned, turning the potatoes halfway through the roasting process. (If the baking sheets do not fit side by side, place one on the middle rack and the other on the bottom rack and rotate the pans once or twice during the roasting process.)

6. Add the greens to the bowl that held the asparagus. Toss with the remaining dressing.

7. Divide the greens among four dinner plates. Arrange the potatoes and asparagus over the greens. Garnish with the cherry tomatoes and serve warm.

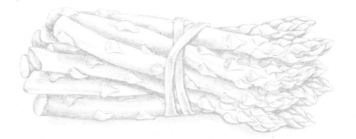

Roasted Beet and Potato Salad

SERVES 4 TO 6

THE COMBINATION OF potatoes, beets, and sour cream is a classic—as wonderful in a salad as it is in borscht. To make this into a main course salad for four, add wedges of hard-cooked eggs and bed the salad on an assortment of greens.

---

3 baking potatoes, such as russet or Idaho, skin on

2 tablespoons extra virgin olive oil

Salt and freshly ground black pepper

3 medium-size beets (about 1 pound), tops and roots trimmed to 1 inch

1 cup sour cream or plain yogurt

½ small red onion, sliced

¼ cup chopped fresh dill

1. Preheat the oven to 425°F. Lightly oil a rimmed baking sheet.

2. Cut the potatoes in half lengthwise. Cut each half into 6 to 8 thin wedges, then cut each wedge in half widthwise. Combine the potatoes, oil, and salt and pepper to taste in a large bowl. Toss to coat. Arrange cut side down in a single layer on the baking sheet.

3. Place the beets in a small baking dish. Cover with aluminum foil.

4. Place the baking sheet and baking dish side by side in the oven. Roast the potatoes for about 25 minutes, until tender and well browned, turning them halfway through the roasting process. Roast the beets for 1 to 1¼ hours, until the largest beet is easily pierced with a knife.

5. Meanwhile, in a small bowl, combine the sour cream, onion, dill, and salt and pepper to taste.

6. When the beets are cool enough to handle, peel and cut into wedges.

7. In a large serving bowl, combine the potatoes and beets. Add the sour cream dressing and mix with a rubber spatula. Serve at once.

Blue Cheese, Roasted Beet, and Endive Salad

SERVES 4 TO 6

WHEN BEETS ARE ROASTED, their flavor is intensified. Add vividly flavored blue cheese and bitter greens, and you have a classic salad to wake up jaded palates.

3 or 4 medium-size beets (about 1 pound), tops and roots trimmed to 1 inch

4 heads Belgian endive, sliced crosswise into 2-inch pieces

2 ounces Roquefort or other blue cheese, crumbled (about ½ cup)

¼ cup slivered almonds or chopped walnuts, toasted (page 211)

½ cup Orange Vinaigrette (page 94)

1. Preheat the oven to 400°F.

2. Place the beets on a large sheet of heavy-duty aluminum foil and wrap to form a well-sealed packet.

3. Roast for 1 to 1¼ hours, until the beets are tender.

4. When the beets are cool enough to handle, peel and cut into 2-inch matchsticks.

5. In a large salad bowl, combine the endive, blue cheese, and nuts. Toss lightly. Add the beets and toss again. Drizzle the dressing over the salad, toss, and serve at once.

Orange Vinaigrette

BEETS HAVE AN AFFINITY for oranges. This delicate dressing is outstanding on any salad that features beets. It is also a great dressing for any green salad that includes strong-tasting greens, such as watercress or escarole.

¼ cup freshly squeezed orange juice

1 teaspoon grated orange zest

2 teaspoons white wine vinegar

½ teaspoon salt

White or freshly ground black pepper

3 tablespoons grapeseed, sunflower, or canola oil

1. In a small bowl, combine the orange juice, orange zest, vinegar, salt, and pepper to taste.

2. Slowly whisk in the oil until emulsified. Taste and adjust the seasonings. Use immediately.

Russian Winter Vegetable Salad

SERVES 6 TO 8

I'M NOT SURE my Russian ancestors ever enjoyed a salad exactly like this, but certainly they ate their share of cabbage and beets. This makes a great meal when combined with baked potatoes and a hearty rye bread.

---

4 to 6 medium-size beets (about 1½ pounds), tops and roots trimmed to 1 inch

1 small head green cabbage (about 2 pounds), quartered, cored, and cut into ½-inch-wide strips

1 onion, halved and thinly sliced

3 tablespoons walnut or peanut oil

2 teaspoons dill seeds

1½ cups sour cream

1 tablespoon chopped fresh dill

¼ cup cider vinegar

Salt and freshly ground black pepper

1. Preheat the oven to 425°F. Lightly oil a large shallow roasting or half sheet pan.

2. Place the beets on a large sheet of heavy-duty aluminum foil and wrap to form a well-sealed packet.

3. In a large bowl, combine the cabbage, onion, oil, and dill seeds. Toss to coat. Arrange in a shallow (preferably single) layer in the pan.

4. Place the beets and cabbage side by side in the oven. Roast the cabbage for 20 to 25 minutes, until very lightly browned and tender, stirring occasionally for even cooking. Do not let the cabbage burn, or it will taste bitter. Roast the beets for 1 to 1¼ hours, until the largest beet is easily pierced with a fork.

5. When the beets are cool enough to handle, peel and cut into thin wedges or slices.

6. Combine the beets and cabbage in a large serving bowl. Add the sour cream, fresh dill, and vinegar. Season generously with salt and pepper. Toss to coat. Serve at room temperature.

Green Bean and Carrot Vinaigrette

SERVES 4 TO 6

THE DRESSING IS a simple combination of olive oil, white balsamic vinegar, and maple syrup and combines deliciously with the roasted vegetables. White balsamic vinegar is misnamed because it is not white at all; it is clear. It is also sometimes hard to find, but well worth the search, since it adds a complex tart-sweet flavor without discoloring the beautiful vegetables.

2 pounds green beans, ends trimmed and cut into 2-inch pieces

1 pound carrots, cut into 2-inch matchsticks

6 tablespoons extra virgin olive oil

Salt and freshly ground black pepper

1 large garlic clove, minced

3 tablespoons white (clear) balsamic vinegar

1 tablespoon pure maple syrup

1. Preheat the oven to 400°F. Lightly oil a large shallow roasting or half sheet pan.

2. In a large bowl, combine the green beans, carrots, and 2 tablespoons of the oil. Toss well to coat. Season with salt and pepper to taste. Arrange in a single layer in the pan.

3. Roast for about 25 minutes, until the vegetables are tender and lightly browned, stirring or shaking the pan a few times for even cooking.

4. In a small bowl, combine the garlic, vinegar, and maple syrup. Whisk in the remaining 4 tablespoons oil until completely emulsified. Season with salt and pepper to taste.

5. Transfer the roasted vegetables to a serving platter. Drizzle the vinaigrette over the vegetables. Serve warm or at room temperature.

Frisée Salad with Warm Lentils, Goat Cheese, and Roasted Onions

SERVES 4 TO 6

FRENCH GREEN LENTILS, or *lentilles du Puy*, are the lentils of choice for this simple combination because they hold their shape so well. Likewise, pearl onions are the best variety to use because of their shape. But for some reason, pearl onions are not readily available except during the holiday season, when you are expected to serve them creamed. This dish looks pretty with whole pearl onions, but you can easily substitute white boiling onions (cut into quarters or eighths if large). Serve with a sauvignon blanc and some crusty French bread, and imagine that you are enjoying lunch in a Parisian bistro.

> 1 pound pearl onions
> 3 tablespoons extra virgin olive oil
> 2 teaspoons fresh thyme leaves
> 1½ cups dried French green lentils, rinsed and picked over
> 2 tablespoons plus 1 teaspoon balsamic vinegar
> 4 ounces mild fresh goat cheese, such as Montrachet, crumbled (about 1 cup)
> Salt and freshly ground black pepper
> 8 to 10 cups torn frisée

1. Preheat the oven to 450°F. Lightly oil a 9 x 13-inch baking dish.

2. Combine the onions, 2 tablespoons of the oil, and thyme in the baking dish. Toss to coat and arrange in a single layer.

3. Roast for 20 to 30 minutes, until the onions are lightly browned, stirring or shaking the pan occasionally for even cooking.

4. Meanwhile, boil the lentils in plenty of salted water until tender but not mushy, about 25 minutes. Drain and transfer to a large bowl.

5. Gently mix the roasted onions into the lentils. Add 2 tablespoons of the vinegar, the goat cheese, and salt and pepper to taste. Toss gently to mix.

6. Toss the frisée with the remaining 1 tablespoon oil and 1 teaspoon vinegar.

7. To serve, arrange the greens on individual dinner plates or on a large serving platter and spoon the lentil and onion mixture on top.

Marinated Roasted Pepper and Olive Salad

SERVES 4 TO 6

THIS IS A TERRIFIC SALAD with any number of serving possibilities. You can make it a meal with the addition of crusty French bread and sliced tomatoes. Or you can serve it as a topping for warm pasta or as a dressing for a cold pasta salad. It also makes a fine addition to an antipasto platter. And if you use pitted olives, you can serve it as a sandwich filling for pita pockets.

2 medium-size green bell peppers

2 medium-size red bell peppers

2 medium-size yellow bell peppers

8 ounces fresh mozzarella cheese, cubed

½ cup brine-cured black olives, such as Kalamata

2 tablespoons extra virgin olive oil

1 tablespoon red wine vinegar

1 tablespoon chopped fresh basil leaves

Salt and freshly ground black pepper

1. Preheat the broiler. Lightly oil a rimmed baking sheet.

2. Place the bell peppers on the baking sheet with space between them. Broil 4 inches from the heat for 10 to 20 minutes, until charred all over, turning several times.

3. Place the peppers in a covered bowl, plastic bag, or paper bag. Seal and let steam for about 10 minutes to loosen the skins.

4. Cut slits in the peppers and drain briefly into a large bowl to catch any juices. Discard the seeds and skins. Cut the peppers into matchsticks and add to the bowl with the pepper juices. Add the mozzarella, olives, oil, vinegar, and basil. Toss to combine. Season with salt and pepper to taste.

5. Let stand for at least 30 minutes to allow the flavors to blend.

6. Serve at room temperature.

Roasted Potato Salad with Herbs and Parmesan Dressing

SERVES 4 TO 6

A GREEN SALAD with substance? Or a potato salad made light with beautiful salad greens? However you describe it, this is a wonderful salad that can form the basis of a light summer meal.

---

2 tablespoons sherry vinegar or red wine vinegar

1 teaspoon Dijon mustard

⅓ cup extra virgin olive oil

Coarse sea salt or kosher salt and freshly ground black pepper

1½ pounds small new potatoes, halved or quartered

1 shallot, minced

¼ cup finely grated Parmigiano-Reggiano cheese

6 cups torn mixed salad greens or mesclun, such as frisée, baby spinach, mizuna, and radicchio

¼ cup chopped mixed fresh herb leaves, such as basil, oregano, marjoram, parsley, thyme, sage, and mint

½ Vidalia or other sweet onion, thinly sliced

2 ripe tomatoes, cut into wedges, for garnish

1. Preheat the oven to 425°F. Lightly oil a rimmed baking sheet.

2. In a small bowl, combine the vinegar and mustard. Slowly drizzle in the oil, whisking until fully emulsified. Season with salt and pepper to taste.

3. Place the potatoes and shallot in a large bowl. Drizzle with 3 tablespoons of the vinaigrette and toss to coat. Arrange in a single layer on the baking sheet.

4. Roast for 30 to 40 minutes, until the potatoes are lightly browned and tender when pierced with a fork, stirring and turning occasionally for even cooking. Sprinkle with half the cheese and toss to coat.

5. Just before serving, in a large serving bowl, combine the greens, herbs, onion, potatoes, and remaining cheese. Toss to mix. Add the remaining vinaigrette and toss to coat. Season with salt and pepper to taste. Garnish with the tomatoes and serve at once.

Roasted Potato and Green Bean Salad

SERVES 4

THE VARIETY OF new potatoes available in the markets in recent years has given new life to potato salad. Look for French marbled (pink and white) potatoes or butter fingerlings and have some fun. This hearty salad can be converted into a satisfying one-dish main course by serving it on a bed of greens.

2 tablespoons white wine vinegar or champagne vinegar

2 garlic cloves, minced

¼ teaspoon Dijon mustard

¼ cup extra virgin olive oil

2 tablespoons chopped fresh chives

Salt and freshly ground black pepper

1 pound green beans, ends trimmed and cut into 2-inch pieces

1½ pounds small new potatoes, halved or quartered

¼ cup thinly sliced red onion

1. Preheat the oven to 425°F. Lightly oil two rimmed baking sheets.

2. In a small bowl, combine the vinegar, garlic, and mustard. Slowly drizzle in the oil, whisking until fully emulsified. Fold in the chives. Season with salt and pepper to taste. Arrange the green beans in a single layer on a baking sheet. Drizzle 2 tablespoons of the vinaigrette over the beans and roll to coat evenly. Place the potatoes on another baking sheet. Drizzle 3 tablespoons of the vinaigrette over the potatoes and turn and toss to coat evenly. Arrange in a single layer.

3. Place the baking sheets side by side in the oven. (If the baking sheets do not fit side by side, place the beans on the bottom rack.) Roast the green beans for about 15 minutes, until well browned and tender, shaking the pan a few times for even cooking. Roast the potatoes for 30 to 40 minutes, until lightly browned and tender when pierced with a fork, stirring or turning occasionally.

4. Transfer the beans and potatoes to a large serving bowl. Add the onion and remaining vinaigrette. Toss to mix well. Season generously with salt and pepper. Serve warm or at room temperature.

Summer Pasta Salad with Roasted Vegetables

SERVES 6 TO 8

A GENEROUS, CROWD-PLEASING SALAD with an abundance of vegetables. It is the contrast between the raw spinach and the sweetly caramelized roasted vegetables that gives this salad so much appeal.

2 small zucchini, cut into matchsticks

2 small yellow summer squash, cut into matchsticks

1 medium-size green bell pepper, cut into matchsticks

1 medium-size red bell pepper, cut into matchsticks

1 large shallot, thinly sliced

¼ cup white (clear) balsamic vinegar

1 tablespoon freshly squeezed lemon juice

1 teaspoon sugar

Salt and freshly ground black pepper

6 tablespoons extra virgin olive oil

1 pound penne, twists, ziti, or other similarly shaped pasta

1 bunch (10 to 12 ounces) fresh spinach, tough stems discarded and leaves torn

1 cup halved cherry tomatoes

½ cup brine-cured black olives, such as Kalamata

¼ cup finely chopped fresh basil leaves

8 ounces fresh mozzarella cheese (optional), cut into ½-inch dice

1. Preheat the oven to 425°F. Lightly oil a large shallow roasting or half sheet pan.

2. In a large bowl, combine the zucchini, summer squash, bell peppers, and shallot. In a small bowl, whisk together the vinegar, lemon juice, sugar, and salt and pepper to taste. Whisk in 5 tablespoons of the oil until fully emulsified. Pour 3 tablespoons of the vinaigrette over the vegetables and toss well. Arrange in a single layer in the pan.

3. Roast for 20 to 25 minutes, until the vegetables are tender and lightly browned, stirring or shaking the pan occasionally for even cooking.

4. Meanwhile, cook the pasta in plenty of boiling salted water until *al dente*. Drain, rinse under cold running water to cool, and transfer to a large bowl. Add

the remaining 1 tablespoon oil and toss to coat. Add the roasted vegetables, spinach, tomatoes, olives, half the basil, and the mozzarella, if using. Toss well.

5. Just before serving, add the remaining vinaigrette and toss again. Season with salt and pepper to taste. Garnish with the remaining basil and serve at room temperature.

Pesto Pasta Salad with Roasted Vegetables

SERVES 4 TO 6

INTENSE FLAVORS ARE the hallmark of this pasta salad. Pesto, olives, garlic, and sweetly roasted vegetables combine to make a memorable dish. The garnish of toasted pine nuts adds a necessary crunch.

3 small zucchini, cut into matchsticks

1 large carrot, cut into matchsticks

1 red bell pepper, cut into matchsticks

4 garlic cloves, slivered

3 tablespoons extra virgin olive oil

Salt and freshly ground black pepper

1 pound bowtie or other short pasta

½ cup pesto, homemade (page 104) or store-bought

2 tablespoons white wine vinegar

½ cup sliced brine-cured black olives, such as Kalamata

2 tablespoons pine nuts, toasted (page 211)

1. Preheat the oven to 425°F. Lightly oil a large shallow roasting or half sheet pan.

2. In a large bowl, combine the zucchini, carrot, bell pepper, and garlic. Add 2 tablespoons of the oil and toss well. Season with salt and pepper to taste. Arrange in a single layer in the pan.

3. Roast for about 20 minutes, until the vegetables are tender and lightly browned, stirring or shaking the pan a few times for even cooking.

4. Meanwhile, cook the pasta in plenty of boiling salted water until *al dente*. Drain, rinse under cold running water to cool, and transfer to a large bowl.

5. Add the remaining 1 tablespoon oil to the pasta and toss to coat. Add the pesto and vinegar and toss again. Add the roasted vegetables and olives and toss once more. Season with salt and pepper to taste.

6. Transfer to a large serving bowl, sprinkle with the pine nuts, and serve at room temperature.

Pesto

PESTO—THE HEAVENLY PASTE made from basil, Parmesan cheese, olive oil, and pine nuts—is an incredibly versatile flavoring agent. If you grow your own basil, it is worth the effort to make pesto and freeze it in small batches to have it available year-round. This is the recipe I use.

1½ cups tightly packed fresh basil leaves
2 garlic cloves, peeled but left whole
3 tablespoons pine nuts, toasted (page 211)
¼ cup extra virgin olive oil
3 tablespoons freshly grated Parmesan cheese
Salt and freshly ground black pepper

1. Combine the basil, garlic, and pine nuts in a food processor. Process until finely chopped.

2. Add the oil through the feed tube with the motor running and continue processing until you have a smooth paste. Briefly mix in the cheese and salt and pepper to taste.

3. Let stand for at least 20 minutes to allow the flavors to develop.

4. Store in an airtight container in the refrigerator for up to 1 week or in the freezer for up to 6 months.

Pasta Salad with Roasted Vegetables and Olive Vinaigrette

SERVES 6 TO 8

IF YOU LOVE OLIVES, you will love this pasta salad. You can use any olives that you have on hand, but be sure to include at least some green olives. Their astringency is a necessary part of the formula.

VEGETABLES AND PASTA

2 small zucchini, cut into matchsticks

1 small yellow summer squash, cut into matchsticks

1 red bell pepper, cut into matchsticks

½ pound green beans, ends trimmed and cut into 1½-inch pieces

½ Vidalia or other sweet onion, halved and slivered

Salt and freshly ground black pepper

3 tablespoons extra virgin olive oil

1 pound penne, twists, ziti, or other similarly shaped pasta

OLIVE VINAIGRETTE

1 cup finely chopped mixed black and green olives

1 tablespoon chopped fresh oregano leaves

2 garlic cloves, minced

2 oil-packed sun-dried tomatoes

¼ cup extra virgin olive oil

⅓ cup freshly squeezed lemon juice (from 1 large lemon), or more to taste

¼ cup finely chopped fresh parsley leaves

1. Preheat the oven to 425°F. Lightly oil a large shallow roasting or half sheet pan.

2. To make the vegetables, in a large bowl, combine the zucchini, summer squash, bell pepper, green beans, and onion. Season generously with salt and pepper. Add 2 tablespoons oil and toss to coat. Arrange in a single layer in the pan.

3. Roast for 20 to 25 minutes, until the vegetables are tender and lightly browned, stirring or shaking the pan occasionally for even cooking.

4. Meanwhile, cook the pasta in plenty of boiling salted water until *al dente*. Drain, rinse under cold running water to cool, and transfer to a large bowl. Add the remaining 1 tablespoon oil and toss to coat.

5. To make the vinaigrette, combine the olives, oregano, garlic, and sun-dried tomatoes in a food processor and pulse until finely chopped. Add the oil and lemon juice and process until well combined.

6. Just before serving, combine the vegetables, pasta, parsley, and dressing and toss to mix. Taste and add more salt, pepper, or lemon juice, if needed. Serve at room temperature.

Pasta Salad Tips I have made a lot of pasta salads in my day, and here is what I know.

- It is a good idea to rinse the pasta under cold running water to remove any starch that remains on the surface of the noodles after the hot water has drained away.

- If you toss freshly cooked pasta with a little olive oil before you combine it with other ingredients, you will seal the pasta, which prevents it from absorbing too much dressing.

- You can make a pasta salad ahead of time by refrigerating the pasta (after tossing it with olive oil), the vegetables, and the dressing in separate containers. Just before serving, toss them together.

- To reduce the fat content of a salad, substitute neutral-tasting chicken or vegetable broth for some of the olive oil. Alternatively, use buttermilk to make a creamy nonfat dressing.

- When making a pasta salad with roasted vegetables, add crunch in the form of nuts, or use a combination of raw and roasted vegetables.

Cold Sesame Noodles with Soy-Roasted Shiitakes

SERVES 4 TO 6

COLD SESAME NOODLES are a standard Chinese menu item. The soy-roasted shiitakes take this familiar dish to new heights. With the addition of the optional vegetable garnishes, you have a delicious main course salad.

SHIITAKES

1½ pounds fresh shiitake mushrooms, stems discarded

¼ cup soy sauce

¼ cup rice vinegar

2 tablespoons mirin (available where Asian foods are sold)

2 garlic cloves, minced

¼ cup toasted sesame oil

4 scallions, white and tender green parts only, sliced

SESAME NOODLES

1 pound fresh Chinese egg noodles or ¾ pound dried

2 tablespoons toasted sesame oil

¼ cup tahini (sesame paste) or natural peanut butter

3 tablespoons soy sauce, or more to taste

1 tablespoon rice vinegar, or more to taste

1 tablespoon sugar, or more to taste

1 teaspoon Chinese chili paste with garlic (available where Asian foods are sold), or more to taste

¼ cup chopped fresh cilantro leaves

OPTIONAL VEGETABLE GARNISHES

1 carrot, cut into long, thin strips

1 cucumber, peeled, seeded, and cut into long, thin strips

¼ pound snow peas, trimmed

1 cup fresh bean sprouts

1. To make the shiitakes, place them in a large bowl. In a small bowl, combine the soy sauce, vinegar, mirin, garlic, and oil. Add to the shiitakes; do not wash the small bowl. Toss to coat. Let stand while you preheat the oven.

2. Preheat the oven to 450°F.

3. Transfer the mushrooms with the remaining marinade to a large shallow roasting pan or half sheet pan. Arrange the mushrooms in a single layer. Do not wash the large bowl.

4. Roast for about 15 minutes, stirring or shaking the pan occasionally for even cooking. Sprinkle the scallions over the mushrooms and roast for another 5 to 10 minutes, until the mushrooms are completely tender and lightly browned.

5. Meanwhile, make the sesame noodles. Cook the noodles in plenty of boiling salted water until *al dente*. Drain well and transfer to the large bowl. Add the oil and toss to coat.

6. In the small bowl, combine the tahini, soy sauce, vinegar, sugar, and chili paste. Whisk to combine. Dip a noodle in the sauce to taste for the seasonings and add more soy sauce, vinegar, sugar, or chili paste as needed.

7. Pour the sauce over the noodles and toss to coat. Add the mushrooms and their juices and the cilantro. Toss again.

8. Transfer the mixture to a large serving bowl or platter. Garnish with any of the vegetables, as desired. Serve at once.

Cranberry-Nut Wild Rice Salad

SERVES 6 TO 8

WILD RICE, WALNUTS, cranberries, and roasted vegetables—a finer, more seasonal salad could not grace a Thanksgiving table.

1½ cups wild rice

4½ cups water

1 teaspoon salt

1 small shallot, minced

3 tablespoons sherry vinegar

½ teaspoon Dijon mustard

1 teaspoon sugar

6 tablespoons walnut oil (see Note)

Salt and freshly ground black pepper

½ pound pearl onions or white boiling onions, halved or quartered if large

1 medium-size fennel bulb, cut into matchsticks and stalks discarded

1 cup walnut pieces

1 cup dried cranberries

1. Rinse the rice in a sieve under cold running water. Drain. In a medium-size saucepan, combine the rice, water, and salt. Cover and bring to a boil, then reduce the heat and simmer for 40 to 60 minutes, until the rice is tender and most of the grains have burst open. Drain off any excess water.

2. To make the vinaigrette, combine the shallot, vinegar, mustard, and sugar in a small bowl. Whisk in the oil until emulsified. Season with salt and pepper to taste.

3. Preheat the oven to 425°F. Lightly oil a large shallow roasting or half sheet pan.

4. In a large bowl, combine the onions and fennel. Add 2 tablespoons of the dressing and toss to coat. Arrange in a single layer in the pan.

5. Roast for 20 to 30 minutes, until the vegetables are just barely browned, stirring or shaking the pan occasionally for even cooking.

6. Meanwhile, spread out the walnuts on a baking sheet. Roast until fragrant, about 5 minutes. Check after a few minutes and remove as soon as the nuts begin to color; do not allow them to scorch.

7. In a large serving bowl, combine the rice, roasted onions and fennel, walnuts, and cranberries. Pour the remaining dressing over the salad and toss to mix. Season with salt and pepper to taste.

8. Chill for at least 1 hour to allow the flavors to blend. If chilling for longer than 1 hour, let the salad lose its chill before serving.

Note: **Walnut oil, at its best, is dark, heavy, and fragrant with walnuts. It makes a superior addition to this salad. Look for walnut oil in natural food and specialty food stores. Like all nut oils, it should be stored in the refrigerator and used within 2 months.**

Peeling Pearl Onions It is a lot easier to peel pearl onions if you first give them a soak in boiling water to loosen the skins. What I like to do is put them in a bowl with boiling water to cover and let them stand while I prepare the other ingredients. By the time the water has cooled enough to put my hands in, the onions are ready to slip out of their skins.

VEGETABLE FEASTS: MAIN DISHES

Winter Vegetable Risotto

RISOTTO IS MADE by slowly stirring broth into rice, coaxing the rice to give up its starchy essence. The rice becomes tender, while the starch blends with the broth to create a creamy sauce. The quality of the broth is very important here—there can be no shortcuts with bouillon cubes. Select a high-quality broth. If it is a vegetable broth, choose one that is neutral (sometimes labeled "un-chicken") in flavor. Many vegetable broths have a dominant tomato, mushroom, or carrot flavor, and those will not work here.

1 medium-size fennel bulb, diced and stalks discarded

1 medium-size red bell pepper, diced

1 small onion, diced

1 small butternut squash (about 1 pound), peeled, seeded, and diced

1 tablespoon chopped fresh rosemary or thyme leaves

5 tablespoons extra virgin olive oil

Salt and freshly ground black pepper

5½ cups high-quality neutral-tasting chicken or vegetable broth

½ cup dry white wine

2 garlic cloves, minced

1½ cups Arborio rice

Freshly grated Parmesan cheese

1. Preheat the oven to 425°F. Lightly oil a large shallow roasting or half sheet pan.

2. In a large bowl, combine the fennel, bell pepper, onion, squash, and rosemary. Add 3 tablespoons of the oil and toss to coat. Season with salt and pepper to taste. Arrange in a single layer in the pan.

3. Roast for 20 to 25 minutes, until the vegetables are lightly browned and tender, stirring once or twice during the cooking.

4. Meanwhile, in a small saucepan over medium heat, combine the broth and wine and heat to simmering.

5. In a large nonstick skillet, heat the remaining 2 tablespoons oil over medium-high heat. Add the garlic and rice and toss to coat. Sauté for 3 to 5 minutes, until the rice appears toasted.

6. Add 1 cup of the simmering broth mixture to the rice and reduce the heat to medium. Cook, stirring, until the broth is mostly absorbed. Continue adding more broth, 1 cup at a time, cooking and stirring as it is absorbed. It will take a total of 18 to 25 minutes for all the broth to be absorbed and the rice to become tender and creamy.

7. Stir the roasted vegetables into the rice. Season to generously with salt and pepper.

8. Serve at once. Pass the Parmesan cheese at the table.

Lemon Risotto with Roasted Summer Vegetables

THE REWARD OF gardening lies in the possibility of going into the garden to pick and clip as needed. In this lemon-scented risotto, the zucchini, summer squash, green beans, and tomatoes are deliciously enhanced by snips of lemon thyme and basil.

2 small zucchini, cut into matchsticks

2 small yellow summer squash, cut into matchsticks

½ pound green beans, ends trimmed and cut into 1½-inch pieces

1 red bell pepper, cut into matchsticks

1 tablespoon chopped fresh lemon thyme or rosemary leaves

4 tablespoons extra virgin olive oil

Salt and freshly ground black pepper

5½ cups high-quality neutral-tasting chicken or vegetable broth

¼ cup dry white wine

¼ cup freshly squeezed lemon juice

1 teaspoon minced lemon zest

2 garlic cloves, minced

1½ cups Arborio rice

¼ cup fresh basil leaves, slivered

1 large ripe tomato, seeded and chopped

¼ cup freshly grated Parmesan cheese

1. Preheat the oven to 425°F. Lightly oil a large shallow roasting or half sheet pan.

2. In a large bowl, combine the zucchini, summer squash, green beans, bell pepper, and lemon thyme. Add 2 tablespoons of the oil and toss to coat. Season with salt and pepper to taste. Arrange in a single layer in the pan.

3. Roast for 25 to 30 minutes, until the vegetables are lightly browned and tender, stirring once or twice for even cooking.

4. Meanwhile, in a small saucepan, combine the broth, wine, lemon juice, and lemon zest. Heat to simmering.

5. In a large nonstick skillet, heat the remaining 2 tablespoons oil over medium-high heat. Add the garlic and rice and toss to coat. Sauté for 3 to 5 minutes, until the rice appears toasted.

6. Add 1 cup of the simmering broth mixture to the rice and reduce the heat to medium. Cook, stirring until the broth is mostly absorbed. Continue adding more broth, 1 cup at a time, cooking and stirring as it is absorbed. It will take a total of 18 to 25 minutes for the broth to be absorbed and the rice to become tender and creamy.

7. Stir the roasted vegetables into the rice. Stir in the basil, tomato, and cheese. Season generously with salt and pepper.

8. Serve at once.

Pecan-Lemon Rice Pilaf with Roasted Asparagus

TOASTED NUTS BRING OUT the nutty subtleties of rice—together they are one of my favorite flavor combinations. For this delicately flavored pilaf, only the most neutral-tasting broth will do. If you do not want to use chicken broth, then use water—most vegetable broths are just too assertive in flavor.

1 pound asparagus (12 to 16 medium-thick spears), bottoms trimmed and cut into
   1½-inch pieces

4 tablespoons extra virgin olive oil

3 tablespoons freshly squeezed lemon juice

Salt and freshly ground black pepper

1 cup pecan pieces

1½ cups basmati or other long-grain white rice

1 shallot, minced

1 garlic clove, minced

2¾ cups high-quality neutral-tasting chicken broth or water

1 teaspoon grated lemon zest

2 tablespoons chopped fresh parsley leaves

1. Preheat the oven to 400°F.

2. In a medium-size bowl, toss the asparagus with 2 tablespoons of the oil and 1 tablespoon of the lemon juice. Season with salt and pepper to taste. Arrange in a single layer on a rimmed baking sheet. Spread out the pecans on a separate baking sheet.

3. Place the baking sheets side by side in the oven. Roast the pecans for 7 to 10 minutes, until fragrant and slightly colored. Roast the asparagus for about 15 minutes, until tender and lightly browned, shaking the pan occasionally for even cooking. (If the baking sheets do not fit side by side, place the pecans on the middle rack and the asparagus on the bottom rack, then transfer the asparagus to the middle rack when the pecans are done.)

4. Meanwhile, place the rice in a colander and rinse under cold running water until the water runs clear. Drain.

5. Heat the remaining 2 tablespoons oil in a large, heavy skillet over medium-high heat. Add the shallot and garlic and sauté for about 2 minutes, until softened. Add the rice and sauté until the rice appears toasted and dry, 3 to 5 minutes. Stir in the broth or water, the remaining 2 tablespoons lemon juice, and the lemon zest. Cover, bring to a boil, reduce the heat to medium, and boil gently for 12 to 15 minutes, until the broth is absorbed and the rice is tender.

6. Fluff the rice with a fork. Stir in the asparagus, pecans, and parsley. Season with salt and pepper to taste. Dry the pot lid and place a crumpled, clean cotton or paper towel on top of the rice to prevent condensed water from dripping back into the pan. Cover with the dried lid and let rest for 5 minutes.

7. Serve immediately.

Spring Casserole of Roasted Asparagus and Artichokes

SERVES 6

THE BRIGHT SPRING FLAVORS of lemon-roasted asparagus and artichokes are grounded by the tangy, salty feta cheese. The vegetables would be delightful on their own but become a satisfying one-dish supper when combined with rice. If you are in the mood, you can replace the rice with orzo.

1¼ to 1½ pounds asparagus (16 to 24 spears), bottoms trimmed and cut into 2-inch pieces

12 canned or frozen and defrosted artichoke hearts, quartered

1 medium-size red bell pepper, cut into matchsticks

2 garlic cloves, minced

2 teaspoons grated lemon zest

Juice of 1 lemon

3 tablespoons extra virgin olive oil

Salt and freshly ground black pepper

1½ cups basmati rice

2¼ cups water

2 cups halved cherry tomatoes

8 ounces feta cheese, crumbled (about 2 cups)

½ cup pitted brine-cured black olives, such as Kalamata

¼ cup chopped fresh parsley leaves

1. Preheat the oven to 425°F. Lightly oil a large shallow roasting or half sheet pan.

2. In a large bowl, combine the asparagus, artichokes, and bell pepper. Add the garlic, lemon zest, lemon juice, oil, and salt and pepper to taste. Toss to coat. Arrange in a single layer in the pan. Do not wash the bowl.

3. Roast for 20 to 25 minutes, until the vegetables are lightly browned and tender, stirring once or twice for even cooking. Remove from the oven and reduce the temperature to 350°F.

4. Meanwhile, in a medium-size saucepan, combine the rice and water. Bring to a boil, cover, reduce the heat, and gently boil for about 12 minutes, until the water is absorbed and the rice is tender.

5. In the large bowl, combine the cooked rice, roasted vegetables, tomatoes, half the cheese, the olives, and parsley. Mix well. Taste and adjust the seasonings.

Transfer to a 2½-quart casserole dish or 9 x 13-inch baking pan. Sprinkle the remaining cheese on top. (The casserole can be made ahead and kept in the refrigerator for up to 4 hours; adjust the baking time if the casserole goes into the oven cold.)

6. Bake for 20 to 30 minutes, until the cheese is melted and the casserole is heated through.

7. Serve hot.

Black Beans and Rice with Fire-Roasted Vegetables

SERVES 4

NOTHING BEATS GOOD OLD rice and beans—unless it is rice and beans topped with chile-fired, cumin-scented vegetables. The fire comes from the chipotle chiles—smoke-dried, ripened jalapeños—and the amount can be adjusted to suit your palate. Tender mouths can eat this with a dollop of sour cream to tame the flame. If you are short on time, substitute a 19-ounce can of black beans for the dried ones, rinse and drain well, and season with ground cumin.

BEANS

1 cup dried black beans, rinsed, picked over, and soaked overnight in water to cover

4 cups water

2 teaspoons ground cumin

1 teaspoon salt

VEGETABLES

1 medium-size red bell pepper, cut into matchsticks

1 medium-size green bell pepper, cut into matchsticks

1 small to medium-size zucchini, cut into matchsticks

1 medium-size onion, halved and slivered

1 cup fresh or frozen corn kernels

3 tablespoons extra virgin olive oil

1 to 2 teaspoons minced chipotles in adobo sauce (see Note)

1 teaspoon ground cumin

Salt and freshly ground black pepper

½ cup homemade or store-bought salsa, or more to taste

Hot cooked white or brown rice

Sour cream

1. Drain the beans. In a medium-size saucepan, combine the beans, water, cumin, and salt. Bring to a boil, then reduce the heat and simmer, partially covered, until the beans are tender, about 1 hour.

2. While the beans cook, preheat the oven to 425°F. Lightly oil a large shallow roasting pan or half sheet pan.

3. To make the vegetables, in a large bowl, combine the bell peppers, zucchini, onion, and corn. In a small bowl, combine the oil, chipotles, and cumin. Pour

over the vegetables and toss to coat. Season with salt and pepper to taste. Arrange in a single layer in the pan.

4. Roast for about 35 minutes, until the vegetables are tender and lightly browned, stirring or shaking the pan occasionally for even cooking.

5. When the beans are tender, drain off the excess water. Combine the beans and the salsa. Taste and adjust the seasonings, adding more salt, pepper, or salsa as needed.

6. To serve, transfer the hot rice to a large serving platter or individual plates. Spoon the beans over the rice. Top with the roasted vegetables. Pass the sour cream at the table.

Note: **Chipotles in adobo sauce are smoked dried jalapeños canned in a vinegar-based sauce. They are found wherever Mexican foods are sold.**

Marinated Vegetable Couscous

SERVES 4

THE FLAVORS OF the Middle East make a rich marinade for the roasted vegetables, which are served on a bed of couscous. This tasty one-dish meal provides the grains, beans, and vegetables for healthy, hearty eating.

6 tablespoons extra virgin olive oil

2 tablespoons red wine vinegar

2 garlic cloves, minced

2 teaspoons ground cumin

½ teaspoon ground cinnamon

2 small zucchini, cut into matchsticks

1 green bell pepper, cut into matchsticks

1 onion, halved and slivered

1 large eggplant (1¾ to 2 pounds), peeled and diced

One 15.5-ounce can chickpeas or 1½ cups cooked chickpeas, rinsed and drained

One 14.5-ounce can diced tomatoes, with their juice

¾ cup tomato juice

¼ cup chopped fresh cilantro leaves

Salt and freshly ground black pepper

1½ cups couscous

2¼ cups boiling water

1. Preheat the oven to 450°F. Lightly oil a large shallow roasting or half sheet pan.

2. In a large bowl, combine the oil, vinegar, garlic, cumin, and cinnamon. Add the zucchini, bell pepper, onion, and eggplant and toss to coat. Arrange in a single layer in the pan.

3. Roast for 30 to 40 minutes, until the vegetables are tender and lightly browned, stirring occasionally for even cooking.

4. Transfer to a large saucepan and add the chickpeas, tomatoes with their juice, and tomato juice. Add the cilantro and salt and pepper to taste. Keep over low heat.

5. Combine the couscous and boiling water in a medium-size bowl. Cover and let steam until all the water is absorbed and the grains are tender, about 10 minutes. Uncover and fluff with a fork.

6. To serve, transfer the couscous to a serving platter. Spoon the vegetables on top and serve hot.

Stacked Roasted Vegetable Enchiladas

S E R V E S   4   T O   6

A HEARTY SUPPER DISH, this is a favorite in my household. The ingredients are easily varied. Different vegetables, different cheese can all be used. Poblano chiles, with their mild but rich flavor, are perfect here, but if you can't find them in the supermarket, substitute other mild to medium-hot chiles, such as jalapeños. Once I even made it with flour tortillas when I realized—at the last minute—that I was out of corn tortillas. They worked. It is a very flexible dish.

2 poblano chiles, cut into matchsticks

1 red bell pepper, cut into matchsticks

1 small to medium-size zucchini, cut into matchsticks

1 medium-size onion, halved and slivered

1 cup fresh or frozen corn kernels

3 tablespoons extra virgin olive oil

1 teaspoon ground cumin

2 garlic cloves, minced

Salt and freshly ground black pepper

½ cup chopped fresh cilantro leaves

2 cups homemade or store-bought salsa

12 corn tortillas, cut into quarters

8 ounces Monterey Jack cheese, grated (about 2 cups)

4 to 6 tablespoons sour cream (nonfat is acceptable)

2 or 3 scallions, white and tender green parts only, finely chopped

1. Preheat the oven to 425°F. Lightly oil a large shallow roasting or half sheet pan.

2. In a large bowl, combine the poblanos, bell pepper, zucchini, onion, and corn. Add the oil, cumin, garlic, and salt and pepper to taste. Toss to coat. Arrange in a single layer in the pan.

3. Roast for 30 to 40 minutes, until the vegetables are tender and lightly browned, stirring or shaking the pan occasionally for even cooking. Remove from the oven and reduce the temperature to 350°F.

4. Lightly oil a 10-inch quiche dish or deep pie plate. Stir the cilantro into the salsa.

5. Pour about ¼ cup of the salsa into the quiche dish and spread with a spoon. Add a layer of tortilla pieces, overlapping them slightly to completely cover the salsa. Top with one-third of the vegetables, then one-quarter of the cheese. Make a second layer of tortillas, salsa, vegetables, and cheese. Top with a another layer of tortillas, salsa, vegetables, and cheese. Cover with a final layer of tortillas, salsa, and cheese. Cover with aluminum foil.

6. Bake for 20 minutes. Remove the foil and bake for another 10 minutes, until the cheese is melted and the dish is heated through.

7. Let sit for 5 minutes, then cut into wedges. Serve topped with a spoonful of sour cream and a sprinkling of scallions.

Soy-Roasted Green Beans, Shiitakes, and Tofu over Rice

SERVES 3 TO 4

IT NEVER FAILS to astonish me how much volume vegetables lose when they are roasted. In this case, a veritable mountain of green beans is reduced to a modest topping for rice. But, don't worry; the flavors are so rich that the dish is eminently satisfying.

1 pound extra-firm or firm tofu

¼ cup soy sauce

2 tablespoons mirin (available where Asian foods are sold)

3 tablespoons toasted sesame oil

2 pounds green beans, ends trimmed

¼ pound fresh shiitake mushrooms, stems discarded and caps sliced

Hot cooked brown or white rice

1. Preheat the oven to 425°F. Lightly oil a rimmed baking sheet and a large shallow roasting pan or half sheet pan.

2. Wrap the tofu in paper towels and squeeze gently to remove excess moisture. Cut the tofu horizontally into three ½-inch-thick slices.

3. Combine the soy sauce and mirin in a large bowl. Whisk in the sesame oil. Brush both sides of the tofu with the soy glaze and arrange on the baking sheet.

4. Add the green beans and shiitakes to the bowl and toss to coat with the remaining glaze. Transfer the vegetables and remaining glaze to the pan and arrange in a single layer.

5. Place the pans side by side in the oven. (If the pans do not fit side by side, place the tofu on the lower rack.) Roast the tofu for about 15 minutes, until browned on both sides, turning once. Roast the green beans and mushrooms for about 30 minutes, until tender and browned, stirring or shaking the pan occasionally for even cooking.

6. Cut the tofu into ½-inch dice and mix into the green beans and mushrooms.

7. Serve immediately over the hot rice.

Chile-Corn Pudding

ROASTING THE CORN and chiles brings out their hidden sweet flavors in this cheesy, rich dish. It makes a delicious main course accompanied by salad—and it is also a good choice for brunch.

Kernels from 6 ears corn (about 3 cups)

2 or 3 fresh green chiles, such as poblanos or jalapeños, seeded and diced

1 medium-size onion, diced

1 small red bell pepper, diced

4 garlic cloves, minced

2 tablespoons extra virgin olive oil

Salt and freshly ground black pepper

4 large eggs

8 ounces Monterey Jack cheese, grated (about 2 cups)

4 ounces sharp cheddar cheese, grated (about 1 cup)

2 tablespoons chopped fresh cilantro leaves

1. Preheat the oven to 450°F. Lightly oil a large shallow roasting or half sheet pan.

2. In a large bowl, combine the corn, chiles, onion, bell pepper, and garlic. Add the oil and toss to coat. Season with salt and pepper to taste. Arrange in a single layer in the pan.

3. Roast for 25 to 30 minutes, until the vegetables are tender and lightly browned, stirring occasionally.

4. Remove from the oven and reduce the temperature to 350°F. Lightly butter a 1½-quart gratin or soufflé dish.

5. In a large bowl, beat the eggs. Add the roasted vegetables, cheeses, cilantro, and salt and pepper to taste. Transfer to the gratin dish.

6. Bake for 25 to 30 minutes, until puffed and golden.

7. This is best served immediately, while it is still hot and puffed, but it can also be served still warm.

Oven-Roasted Ratatouille

SERVES 6

IN THE PERFECT RATATOUILLE, the flavors are blended, yet each vegetable remains distinct. The vegetables are neither mushy nor undercooked. Despite the fact that ratatouille is traditionally cooked on top of the stove, roasting can bring you closest to perfection. Because roasting is a dry-heat process, the vegetables can be well cooked without steaming into mush. How well the flavors are blended is the test of your cooking skills. But here is a tip: let the ratatouille stand at room temperature for an hour or two to allow the flavors to blend. Taste and adjust the seasoning before serving.

2 medium-size eggplants (about 3 pounds), peeled and cut into ⅓-inch dice

2 medium-size zucchini, diced

2 medium-size yellow summer squash, diced

2 medium-size onions, diced

1 medium-size green bell pepper, diced

1 medium-size red bell pepper, diced

8 garlic cloves, thinly sliced

6 tablespoons extra virgin olive oil

2 tablespoons chopped fresh oregano leaves

Salt and freshly ground black pepper

One 28-ounce can peeled Italian tomatoes, with their juice

¼ cup chopped fresh basil leaves

1 tablespoon capers, drained

1. Preheat the oven to 425°F. Lightly oil two large shallow roasting pans or two half sheet pans.

2. In a large bowl, combine the eggplant, zucchini, summer squash, onions, bell peppers, and garlic. Add the oil, oregano, and salt and pepper to taste. Toss to coat. Arrange in a single layer in the pans.

3. Place the pans on the middle and lower racks of the oven. Roast for 30 to 40 minutes, until the vegetables are lightly browned and tender, occasionally stirring or shaking the pans and rotating them for even cooking.

4. Cut the tomatoes into 1-inch pieces or use your hands to break them up. Place in a large bowl along with their juice. Add the roasted vegetables, basil, and capers. Taste and adjust the seasonings, adding salt and pepper as needed.

5. If possible, allow the ratatouille to stand for up to 2 hours.

6. Serve at room temperature or reheat gently to serve warm.

Roasted Chiles Rellenos

THE CHILES RELLENOS served in most Mexican restaurants are deep-fried. In this simpler, homier version, the batter is baked on top of the cheese-stuffed chiles. Poblanos are the chiles of choice here, prized for their mildly spicy, somewhat fruity flavor and thick flesh.

8 medium-size poblano chiles

8 ounces Monterey Jack cheese, shredded (about 2 cups)

5 large eggs, separated

1 tablespoon plus 1 teaspoon unbleached all-purpose flour

½ teaspoon salt

Warm flour tortillas

Homemade or store-bought salsa

1. Preheat the broiler. Lightly oil a rimmed baking sheet.

2. Place the chiles on the baking sheet with space between them. Broil 4 inches from the heat for 10 to 15 minutes, until blistered and charred, turning as needed for even roasting. Reduce the oven temperature to 350°F.

3. Place the chiles in a covered bowl, plastic bag, or paper bag. Seal and let steam for about 10 minutes to loosen the skins. Cut a 2-inch-long slit in the side of each chile and remove the seeds. Discard the seeds and skins. Set the chiles aside.

4. Lightly oil a baking dish just large enough to hold the chiles in a single layer. Pack the cheese firmly into the chiles and place in the baking dish.

5. Beat the egg yolks with the flour and salt in a medium-size bowl. In another bowl, beat the egg whites with an electric mixer until soft peaks form. Gently fold the whites into the yolks. Spread the egg batter over the chiles.

6. Bake for about 15 minutes, until the topping is browned.

7. Serve hot, passing the tortillas and salsa at the table.

Pesto Eggplant Rollatine

SERVES 4

GARLIC-SCENTED ROASTED EGGPLANT slices are slathered with pesto, filled with cheese, and baked on a bed of tomato sauce. The trick is to cut the eggplants into uniform slices so they cook evenly. A simple pasta dressed with butter and cheese or olive oil and garlic makes a nice accompaniment.

---

3 tablespoons extra virgin olive oil

2 garlic cloves, minced

2 medium-size eggplants (about 3 pounds), peeled and sliced lengthwise into ⅜-inch-thick steaks

Salt and freshly ground black pepper

2 cups well-seasoned tomato sauce

1 cup pesto, homemade (page 104) or store-bought

4 ounces mozzarella cheese, grated (about 1 cup)

1 cup freshly grated Parmesan cheese

1. Preheat the oven to 400°F. Lightly oil two rimmed baking sheets.

2. Combine the oil and garlic. Brush on both sides of the eggplant slices. Arrange in a single layer on the baking sheets. Season generously with salt and pepper.

3. Place the baking sheets side by side in the oven. Roast for 20 to 25 minutes, until well browned and very tender, turning once. Remove from the oven and reduce the temperature to 350°F. (If the baking sheets do not fit side by side, place one on the middle rack and the other on the bottom rack and rotate them once or twice during the roasting process.)

4. Spread about 1 cup of the sauce in the bottom of a 9 x 13-inch baking dish. Spread each eggplant slice with pesto and top with a couple of tablespoons of each cheese. Roll up and place seam side down in the baking dish. Spoon the remaining sauce over the rolls. Sprinkle with the remaining cheese.

5. Bake for about 15 minutes, until the cheese is melted and the eggplant is heated through.

6. Serve hot.

Roasted Vegetable Cutlets

ROASTED VEGETABLES CONTRIBUTE the flavor, while tofu gives the cutlets their heft and protein. The trick is to freeze the tofu first—still in its plastic tub—then defrost it. In the freezing process, water will be forced out of the tofu. Once defrosted, the tofu can be crumbled and made into burgers or cutlets, without the addition of a lot of binders.

1 small eggplant (about 1 pound), peeled and cubed

½ pound green beans, ends trimmed and cut into 2-inch pieces

2 medium-size carrots, sliced

1 medium-size onion, diced

8 garlic cloves, peeled but left whole

3 tablespoons toasted sesame oil

Salt and freshly ground black pepper

1 pound extra-firm or firm tofu, frozen and defrosted

2 tablespoons tahini (sesame paste)

3 tablespoons Tamari-Roasted Sunflower Seeds (page 212) or toasted sunflower seeds (page 211)

1 cup soft whole wheat bread crumbs (about 2 slices)

2 to 3 tablespoons canola oil

1. Preheat the oven to 450°F. Lightly oil a large shallow roasting or half sheet pan.

2. In a large bowl, combine the eggplant, green beans, carrots, onion, and garlic. Add the sesame oil and toss to coat. Season with salt and pepper to taste. Arrange in a single layer in the pan. Do not wash the bowl.

3. Roast for about 30 minutes, until the vegetables are tender and well browned, stirring or shaking the pan occasionally. Remove from the oven and reduce the temperature to 250°F.

4. Meanwhile, crumble the tofu into a colander. Drain well.

5. Transfer the roasted vegetables to a cutting board and finely chop. Transfer to the large bowl and add the crumbled tofu, tahini, sunflower seeds, and bread crumbs. Season with salt and pepper to taste. Form the mixture into 8 patties and refrigerate for at least 30 minutes.

6. Heat the canola oil in a large skillet over medium-high heat. Add half the patties to the skillet. Fry until golden on both sides, about 4 minutes per side. Keep hot in the oven while you fry the remaining patties.

7. Serve hot.

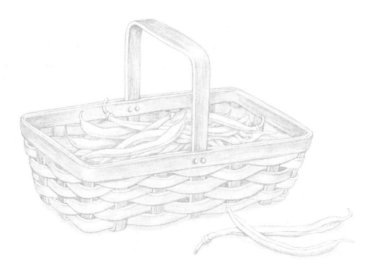

Stuffed Portobello Stacks

SERVES 4

STUFFED PORTOBELLO MUSHROOMS must be to vegetarians what an expensive cut of red meat is to carnivores—a rich, indulgent feast. In this case, it is a feast without guilt. The creamy tang of goat cheese is a wonderful foil for the earthy mushrooms. Basil and fresh tomato keep the flavors bright.

8 portobello mushrooms

4 tablespoons extra virgin olive oil

2 shallots, minced

2 garlic cloves, minced

8 ounces mild fresh goat cheese, such as Montrachet

8 fresh basil leaves

8 large ripe tomato slices

3 tablespoons dry bread crumbs

1. Preheat the oven to 500°F. Lightly oil a rimmed baking sheet.

2. Carefully remove the stems from the mushrooms and reserve. Brush both sides of the caps with 3 tablespoons of the oil. Place the caps rounded side up on the baking sheet.

3. Roast for 6 minutes. Turn the mushrooms over and roast for about another 4 minutes, until cooked through.

4. Meanwhile, finely chop the mushroom stems. Heat the remaining 1 tablespoon oil in a small sauté pan over medium-high heat. Add the mushroom stems, shallots, and garlic. Sauté for 6 minutes, until the stems are well browned.

5. Gently spread each roasted mushroom cap with a portion of the goat cheese and top with the sautéed mushroom mixture. Add a basil leaf and a tomato slice to each. Sprinkle a light coating of crumbs on top. (The mushrooms can be held in the refrigerator for up to 4 hours. Bring to room temperature before returning to the oven.)

6. Roast for about 5 minutes, until heated through.

7. Serve hot.

SENSATIONAL SANDWICHES AND WRAPS

Roasted Vegetable Muffuletta

Pesto and Roasted Vegetable Loaf

Marinated Roasted Vegetable Subs

Cumin-Scented Roasted Vegetable Roll-Ups
with Hummus

Greek Salad Pita Pockets with Roasted
Eggplant Slices

Roasted Eggplant Roll-Ups with Tzatziki

Roasted Eggplant-Garlic Roll-Ups

Mushroom Steak Sandwiches with
Roquefort Dressing

Goat Cheese and Artichokes on Focaccia

Italian-Style Roasted Vegetable Subs

Vegetarian Fajitas

Barbecued Tempeh Sandwiches with Creamy Slaw

Roasted Vegetable Muffuletta

A HERO OF A SANDWICH, this sublime combination of intensely flavored olives and roasted vegetables is almost without equal in the world of sandwiches. The New Orleans original is loaded with meat, but the signature flavor comes from the olive relish that permeates each bite. This may be a humble sandwich, but packed along on a picnic (don't forget the napkins), it is the ultimate in food-to-go. Note that the olive relish must be made in advance to allow time for the flavors to blend.

OLIVE RELISH

1 roasted red pepper (page 42), finely chopped

½ cup finely chopped brine-cured green olives, such as Picholine

½ cup finely chopped brine-cured black olives, such as Kalamata

½ cup finely chopped celery

¼ cup finely chopped fresh parsley leaves

2 teaspoons finely chopped fresh oregano leaves

1 garlic clove, minced

¼ cup extra virgin olive oil

¼ cup freshly squeezed lemon juice

VEGETABLES

1 large eggplant (1¾ to 2 pounds), peeled and sliced lengthwise into ⅜-inch-thick steaks

5 tablespoons extra virgin olive oil

1 medium-size onion, halved and slivered

1 medium-size red or green bell pepper, cut into matchsticks

¼ pound mushrooms, trimmed and chopped

ASSEMBLY

1 large (8- to 10-inch) round loaf Italian or French bread

⅓ pound provolone cheese, sliced

1. To make the relish, combine all the ingredients in a medium-size bowl. Mix well. Cover and refrigerate for at least 8 hours or up to 4 days.

2. Preheat the oven to 400°F. Lightly oil two rimmed baking sheets.

3. To prepare the vegetables, arrange the eggplant slices in a single layer on one baking sheet and brush them on both sides with 3 tablespoons of the oil.

Arrange the onion, bell pepper, and mushrooms in a single layer on the second baking sheet and drizzle with the remaining 2 tablespoons oil.

4. Place the baking sheets side by side in the oven. Roast for 10 minutes; turn the eggplant over and stir the onion mixture. Roast for about another 10 minutes, until the vegetables are browned and tender. (If the baking sheets do not fit side by side, place one on the middle rack and the other on the bottom rack and rotate them once or twice during the roasting process.)

5. To assemble the sandwich, cut the bread in half horizontally and remove most of the soft white center. Generously slather the inside of the bottom of the loaf with half the relish. Arrange half the provolone on the bread. Cover the provolone with one-third of the eggplant and then half of the onion, pepper, and mushrooms. Add another layer of eggplant, the remaining vegetables, and then the remaining eggplant. Top with the remaining provolone. Slather the inside of the top of the loaf with the remaining relish and place firmly on the bottom.

6. If you are planning to serve the loaf cold, wrap in plastic wrap and let sit for 30 minutes, or up to 4 hours. To serve warm, preheat the oven to 300°F, wrap the loaf in aluminum foil, and bake for about 15 minutes, until the cheese is melted.

Pesto and Roasted Vegetable Loaf

SERVES 4 TO 6

TAKE A LOAF of crusty French bread, dress it with pesto, stuff it with roasted vegetables, and meld it together with melted cheese, and you have the perfect fare for a picnic or casual alfresco meal. The sandwich can be made ahead of time and quickly reheated in the oven or even over a campfire.

5 tablespoons extra virgin olive oil

3 garlic cloves, minced

1 medium-size eggplant (about 1½ pounds), peeled and sliced into ⅜-inch-thick rounds

2 medium-size portobello mushrooms, trimmed and caps sliced

1 small to medium-size zucchini, cut into matchsticks

1 medium-size red bell pepper, cut into matchsticks

Salt and freshly ground black pepper

1 large loaf Italian or French country bread or focaccia (1¼- to 1½-pound loaf)

½ cup pesto, homemade (page 104) or store-bought

⅓ pound provolone cheese, sliced

2 large ripe tomatoes

1. Preheat the oven to 425°F. Lightly oil two rimmed baking sheets.

2. Combine the olive oil and garlic in a small bowl. Brush the oil mixture on both sides of the eggplant slices and arrange in a single layer on one of the baking sheets.

3. In a medium-size bowl, combine the mushrooms, zucchini, and bell pepper. Add the remaining garlic oil and salt and pepper to taste. Toss to coat. Arrange in a single layer on the second baking sheet.

4. Place the baking sheets side by side in the oven. Roast for about 20 minutes, until all the vegetables are well browned and tender, turning the eggplant once and stirring the other vegetables once or twice for even cooking. (If the baking sheets do not fit side by side, place one on the middle rack and the other on the bottom rack and rotate them once or twice during the roasting process.) Remove from the oven and reduce the temperature to 300°F.

5. Cut the bread in half horizontally. Remove some of the interior of the loaf to create a hollow space for the vegetables. Spread the pesto inside both halves of

the loaf. Beginning and ending with the cheese, layer the cheese, roasted vegetables, and tomatoes on the bread. Place the top half of the loaf on the bottom and wrap in aluminum foil.

6. Bake for 10 minutes, until the bread is lightly toasted and the cheese is melted.

7. To serve, unwrap the loaf and slice into wedges or squares. Serve hot.

Note: **The loaf can be assembled up to 1 day in advance and refrigerated in its foil wrapper. To heat, increase the baking time to about 30 minutes, turning occasionally.**

Variations on a Theme Possible variations on this theme are infinite. Substitute Olive Relish (page 136) for the pesto. Use different vegetables, replacing some or all of the ones specified with yellow summer squash, green beans, or asparagus. Cheddar, fontina, Monterey Jack, Colby, Gouda—any semihard cheese with good melting properties—can replace the provolone. Or use goat cheese and omit the pesto and provolone.

Marinated Roasted Vegetable Subs

SERVES 4

THIS DELICATE MIX of summer vegetables is nicely enhanced by a light herbal marinade and mild fontina cheese. Choose any single herb or a mix of herbs. I have a large herb garden and like to snip an assortment for these vegetables—lemon basil and lemon thyme are particularly agreeable. This very simple combination makes a great light meal.

6 canned or frozen and defrosted artichoke hearts, quartered

3 Belgian endives, trimmed and cut into ¼-inch-wide strips

2 medium-size zucchini, cut into matchsticks

1 large leek, white and tender green parts only, thinly sliced

1 large red bell pepper, cut into matchsticks

¼ cup extra virgin olive oil

1 tablespoon plus 1 teaspoon red wine vinegar

2 garlic cloves, minced

3 tablespoons chopped fresh basil, oregano, rosemary, thyme, or mint leaves

Salt and freshly ground black pepper

4 submarine rolls or petite baguettes

⅓ pound fontina cheese, thinly sliced

1. Preheat the oven to 450°F. Lightly oil a large shallow roasting or half sheet pan.

2. In a large bowl, combine the artichoke hearts, endives, zucchini, leek, and bell pepper. In a small bowl, whisk together the oil, vinegar, garlic, and herb. Season with salt and pepper to taste. Pour the marinade over the vegetables and toss to coat well. Remove the vegetables from the marinade with a slotted spoon and arrange in a shallow (preferably single) layer in the pan.

3. Roast for about 25 minutes, until the vegetables are tender and lightly browned, tossing and turning occasionally for even cooking. Remove the vegetables from the oven and reduce the temperature to 300°F.

4. To assemble the subs, cut the rolls open horizontally (do not cut all the way through). Brush a little of the remaining marinade inside. Stuff each roll with vegetables. Divide the cheese among the rolls and stuff into the subs. Close the subs so that as little cheese as possible peeks out. Tightly wrap each sandwich in aluminum foil.

5. Bake for about 15 minutes, until the rolls are crispy and the cheese is melted.

6. Serve warm.

Bread: The Bottom Line There is no point in going to the trouble of roasting vegetables unless you can sandwich them between slices of truly great bread. Look for artisanal loaves from bakeries and avoid any bread wrapped in plastic. It just won't do justice to your sweet, tasty vegetables.

Cumin-Scented Roasted Vegetable Roll-Ups with Hummus

SERVES 4

HUMMUS—THE MIDDLE EASTERN SPREAD of chickpeas and tahini—makes an inspired sandwich with roasted vegetables. If you have the time, make the hummus first to let the flavors fully develop. If you are pressed for time, you can whip up the hummus while the vegetables roast. And more choices: you can roll the hummus and vegetables in lavash or another flatbread, or you can stuff the combo into pita pockets. This recipe is terrific any way you serve it.

HUMMUS

2 garlic cloves, peeled but left whole

¼ cup fresh parsley leaves

One 15.5-ounce can chickpeas or 1½ cups cooked chickpeas, rinsed and drained

¼ cup tahini (sesame paste)

3 tablespoons freshly squeezed lemon juice

Salt and freshly ground black pepper

ROLL-UPS

⅓ cup extra virgin olive oil

2 garlic cloves, minced

2 teaspoons ground cumin

1 small eggplant (about 1 pound), peeled and sliced into ⅜-inch-thick rounds

1 small zucchini, cut into matchsticks

1 onion, halved and slivered

1 green bell pepper, cut into matchsticks

1 red bell pepper, cut into matchsticks

4 pieces lavash, other flatbread, or pita pockets

1. To make the hummus, combine the garlic and parsley in a food processor. Process until finely chopped. Add the chickpeas, tahini, and lemon juice and process until smooth. Add 1 tablespoon water and process until the hummus is light and smooth. If needed, add up to 3 tablespoons water total. Season with salt and pepper to taste. Set aside.

2. Preheat the oven to 425°F. Lightly oil two rimmed baking sheets.

3. To make the roll-ups, combine the oil, garlic, and cumin in a small bowl. Brush both sides of the eggplant slices with the flavored oil and arrange in a single

layer on one of the baking sheets. In a medium-size bowl, combine the zucchini, onion, and bell peppers. Add the remaining flavored oil and toss to coat. Arrange in a single layer on the second baking sheet.

4. Place the baking sheets side by side in the oven. Roast for 10 minutes, turn the eggplant over, and stir the onion-pepper mixture, and then roast for another 10 minutes, until the vegetables are well browned and tender. (If the baking sheets do not fit side by side, place one on the middle rack and the other on the bottom rack and rotate them once or twice during the roasting process.)

5. To assemble the roll-ups, divide the hummus among the lavash, spreading it evenly to within an inch of the edges. Place the eggplant slices on the hummus, top with the mixed vegetables, and roll up to enclose the filling. Or stuff the hummus and vegetables into pita pockets.

6. Serve at once or wrap in plastic wrap or aluminum foil and tuck into a picnic basket or lunch box.

Greek Salad Pita Pockets with Roasted Eggplant Slices

SERVES 4 TO 6

MARINATING TOMATOES IN olive oil and lemon juice brings out their flavor whether you are making this wonderful combination in midwinter or midsummer. This is a great way to make a meal out of a Greek salad.

GREEK SALAD

1 large head romaine lettuce, torn into bite-size pieces

½ English cucumber, sliced

2 large ripe tomatoes, chopped

1 Vidalia or other sweet onion, thinly sliced

2 tablespoons extra virgin olive oil

2 tablespoons freshly squeezed lemon juice

2 tablespoons chopped fresh mint leaves

½ cup brine-cured black olives, such as Kalamata

4 ounces feta cheese, crumbled (about 1 cup)

SANDWICHES

¼ cup extra virgin olive oil

1 tablespoon chopped fresh oregano leaves

Salt and freshly ground black pepper

2 pounds eggplant (preferably Japanese or Chinese), peeled and sliced into ⅜-inch-thick rounds

6 pita pockets

1. To make the salad, combine the lettuce and cucumber in a large salad bowl, cover, and refrigerate. In a medium-size bowl, combine the tomatoes, onion, oil, lemon juice, mint, olives, and cheese. Set aside at room temperature.

2. Preheat the oven to 400°F. Lightly oil two rimmed baking sheets.

3. To make the sandwiches, combine the oil, oregano, and salt and pepper to taste. Brush both sides of the eggplant slices with the flavored oil and arrange in a single layer on the baking sheets.

4. Place the baking sheets side by side in the oven. Roast for 20 to 25 minutes, until the eggplant is well browned and very tender, turning once. (If the baking sheets do not fit side by side, place one on the middle rack and the other on the

bottom rack and rotate them once or twice during the roasting process.) Remove from the oven and turn off the heat.

5. Wrap the pita pockets in aluminum foil and place in the oven to warm.

6. Add the marinated tomato mixture to the salad bowl and toss to combine.

7. Serve the warmed pita pockets, roasted eggplant, and Greek salad at the table, allowing the diners to assemble their own sandwiches.

Roasted Eggplant Roll-Ups with Tzatziki

SERVES 6

THESE ROLL-UPS ARE a handful of flavor, with the roasted eggplant providing the substance of the sandwich. Season generously with salt and pepper and be sure to provide extra napkins.

TZATZIKI

2 English cucumbers, quartered lengthwise and thinly sliced

2 cups plain yogurt

¼ cup chopped fresh mint leaves

6 garlic cloves, minced

¼ cup extra virgin olive oil

2 tablespoons white or red wine vinegar

Salt and freshly ground black pepper

ROLL-UPS

4 large ripe tomatoes, quartered and sliced

1 cup thinly sliced Vidalia or other sweet onion

5 tablespoons extra virgin olive oil

2 tablespoons red wine vinegar

Salt and freshly ground black pepper

2 medium-size eggplants (about 3 pounds), peeled and sliced into ⅜-inch-thick rounds

6 pieces lavash or other flatbread

1. To make the tzatziki, combine the cucumbers, yogurt, mint, garlic, oil, and vinegar. Season generously with salt and pepper. Set aside at room temperature to allow the flavors to develop.

2. To make the roll-ups, combine the tomatoes and onion in a medium-size bowl. Add 2 tablespoons of the oil and the vinegar and toss to coat. Season generously with salt and pepper and set aside at room temperature to allow the flavors to blend.

3. Preheat the oven to 400°F. Brush two rimmed baking sheets with oil.

4. Brush both sides of the eggplant slices with the remaining 3 tablespoons oil and arrange in a single layer on the baking sheets. Season generously with salt and pepper.

5. Place the baking sheets side by side. Roast for 20 to 25 minutes, until the eggplant is well browned and very tender, turning once. (If the baking sheets do not fit side by side, place one on the middle rack and the other on the bottom rack and rotate them once or twice during the roasting process.)

6. To assemble the roll-ups, spread each lavash with the tzatziki mixture. Arrange the eggplant down the center of each lavash. Top with a few tablespoons of the tomato mixture and roll up.

7. Serve at once, passing any extra tomatoes and tzatziki at the table.

Roasted Eggplant-Garlic Roll-Ups

SERVES 4 TO 6

EACH BITE OF this flavorful wrap is loaded with flavors. The roasted garlic adds depth to the Middle Eastern–style eggplant spread, while the cilantro-laced tomato relish adds fruity, floral flavor notes. This makes a great casual supper, accompanied by roasted potatoes.

EGGPLANT SPREAD

1 large eggplant (1 ¾ to 2 pounds)

¼ cup lightly packed fresh flat-leaf parsley leaves

2 heads Roasted Garlic (page 30) or 2 tablespoons Garlic Puree (page 28)

3 tablespoons freshly squeezed lemon juice, or more to taste

2 tablespoons tahini (sesame paste)

1 teaspoon salt, or more to taste

Freshly ground black pepper

TOMATO-CILANTRO RELISH

1 large ripe tomato, finely chopped

¼ cup finely chopped Vidalia or other sweet onion

¼ cup chopped fresh cilantro leaves

2 tablespoons extra virgin olive oil

2 teaspoons red wine vinegar

Salt and freshly ground black pepper

ASSEMBLY

4 to 6 pieces lavash or other flatbread

4 to 6 romaine lettuce leaves

1. Preheat the oven to 400°F.

2. To make the spread, prick the eggplant with a fork in several places on all sides. Place on a baking sheet and roast for 40 to 60 minutes, until the eggplant is completely soft and collapsed, turning occasionally.

3. Place the eggplant in a colander, slice open with a knife, and let drain and cool for about 30 minutes.

4. In a food processor, finely chop the parsley. Remove the eggplant flesh from the skin and add the flesh to the food processor. Squeeze the roasted garlic from the skins and add to the food processor (or just add the puree), along with the

lemon juice, tahini, salt, and pepper to taste. Process until fairly smooth. Taste and adjust the seasonings, adding more salt, pepper, or lemon juice as needed.

5. Cover and let stand for at least 30 minutes to allow the flavors to blend.

6. Meanwhile, make the relish. In a medium-size bowl, combine the tomato, onion, cilantro, oil, vinegar, and salt and pepper to taste. Set aside to allow the flavors to blend.

7. To assemble the roll-ups, spread one-quarter of the eggplant spread on each piece of lavash. Spoon a few tablespoons of the tomato mixture on the eggplant. Add a lettuce leaf and roll up to enclose the filling. Repeat with the remaining ingredients.

8. Serve at once.

Mushroom Steak Sandwiches with Roquefort Dressing

SERVES 4

IN THE REALM of vegetarian sandwiches, portobello mushrooms hold an honored place. Their wonderfully dense texture and earthy flavor give weight and heft to a sandwich, replacing the ubiquitous slice of cheese. If you want to take these sandwiches on a picnic, roast the mushrooms and prepare the dressing in advance, but assemble the sandwiches just before eating.

BLUE CHEESE DRESSING

¼ cup buttermilk

3 tablespoons crumbled Roquefort or other blue cheese

2 tablespoons mayonnaise (reduced fat is fine)

2 tablespoons chopped fresh parsley leaves

1 garlic clove, peeled but left whole

MUSHROOM SANDWICHES

4 large portobello mushrooms, trimmed and caps sliced ½ inch thick

Extra virgin olive oil

8 large slices high-quality white or whole wheat bread

4 slices Vidalia or other sweet onion

1 ripe tomato, sliced

1 bunch arugula or watercress, stemmed, or 2 cups mesclun

1. Make the dressing by combining the buttermilk, cheese, mayonnaise, parsley, and garlic in a blender or food processor. Process until thick and fairly smooth. Set aside at room temperature to let the flavors develop.

2. Preheat the oven to 500°F. Lightly oil two rimmed baking sheets.

3. To make the sandwiches, lightly brush both sides of the mushroom slices with oil. Arrange in a single layer on the baking sheets.

4. Place the baking sheets side by side in the oven. Roast for about 10 minutes. Turn and roast for about another 10 minutes, until the mushrooms are completely tender when pierced with a fork. (If the baking sheets do not fit side by side, place one on the middle rack and the other on the bottom rack and rotate them once or twice during the roasting process.) Remove from the oven but leave the oven on.

5. Place the bread directly on the oven rack and toast briefly.

6. To assemble the sandwiches, spread the dressing on the bread. Arrange the mushrooms on 4 slices. Add an onion slice to each. Top with the tomato and greens. Cover with the remaining slices of bread. Cut in half, if desired.

7. Serve at once.

Mushroom Steak Sandwiches with Goat Cheese Dressing: **Replace the blue cheese in the dressing with mild fresh goat cheese, such as Montrachet. Proceed with the recipe as above.**

Blue Cheese Dressing Notes The blue cheese dressing can be made several days in advance and stored in an airtight jar in the refrigerator. In fact, the dressing can be made in double or triple batches and used as a salad dressing. It also makes a great dip for raw vegetables.

Goat Cheese and Artichokes on Focaccia

SERVES 6

IF YOU START with store-bought focaccia, this sandwich takes very little time to throw together because it uses bottled marinated artichoke hearts. If the focaccia is lightly seasoned, the garlic butter topping is a tasty way to bring all the flavors together. But some focaccia come freighted with cheese, herbs, and garlic. If that is the case, skip the topping—it will be delicious without the gilding.

FOCACCIA

Three 6-ounce jars marinated artichoke hearts

2 tablespoons chopped fresh basil, oregano, or thyme leaves

One 10-inch focaccia, cut in half horizontally

8 ounces mild fresh goat cheese, such as Montrachet, at room temperature

1 roasted red bell pepper (page 42), cut into strips

OPTIONAL TOPPING

¼ cup (½ stick) butter, melted

2 garlic cloves, minced

1. Preheat the oven to 425°F.

2. To make the focaccia, pour the artichoke hearts and marinade into a 9 x 13-inch baking pan and arrange the artichokes in a single layer. Sprinkle the herbs over the artichokes.

3. Roast for about 15 minutes, until the artichokes are lightly browned and fragrant. Remove from the oven but leave the oven on.

4. Brush the cut sides of the focaccia with the marinade remaining in the pan. Spread the goat cheese on the bottom half. Lift the artichokes out of the marinade with a slotted spoon and arrange on the goat cheese. Top with the pepper. Place the top half of the focaccia on top of the vegetables to close the sandwich.

5. If desired, combine the melted butter and garlic. Brush the garlic butter on top of the sandwich.

6. Place the focaccia on a baking sheet and bake for 10 to 15 minutes, until the top is lightly toasted.

7. Slice into wedges or squares and serve warm.

Italian-Style Roasted Vegetable Subs

SERVES 4

A VEGETARIAN VERSION of the ever-popular meatball sub. These are great for fall picnics, and the recipe can be multiplied easily to feed a crowd.

---

1 pound mushrooms (preferably portobellos), trimmed and sliced

1 large onion, thinly sliced

1 large green bell pepper, cut into matchsticks

1 large red bell pepper, cut into matchsticks

¼ cup Italian-style salad dressing

2 tablespoons extra virgin olive oil

Salt and freshly ground black pepper

4 submarine rolls or petite baguettes

2 cups well-seasoned tomato sauce, homemade (page 62) or store-bought, heated

¼ pound provolone cheese, thinly sliced

1. Preheat the oven to 450°F. Lightly oil a large shallow roasting or half sheet pan.

2. In a large bowl, combine the mushrooms, onion, and bell peppers. Add the salad dressing and oil. Toss to coat. Season with salt and pepper to taste. Arrange in a single layer in the pan.

3. Roast for about 25 minutes, until the vegetables are tender and lightly browned, tossing and turning occasionally for even cooking. Remove from the oven and reduce the temperature to 300°F.

4. To assemble the subs, cut the rolls open horizontally (do not cut all the way through). Brush a little tomato sauce inside. Stuff each roll with vegetables. Cover with sauce, about ½ cup per roll. Divide the cheese among the rolls and stuff into the subs. Close the subs so that as little cheese as possible peeks out. Tightly wrap each sandwich in aluminum foil.

5. Bake for about 15 minutes, until the rolls are crispy and the cheese is melted.

6. Serve warm, with plenty of napkins.

Vegetarian Fajitas

CUMIN-SCENTED ROASTED EGGPLANT is the star in these wraps, but the supporting players—tomatoes, avocados, bell pepper, and onion—must be given their due. For vegetable lovers, these fajitas are pure pleasure.

5 tablespoons extra virgin olive oil

1 tablespoon ground cumin

2 garlic cloves, minced

Salt and freshly ground black pepper

1 large or 2 small eggplants (about 2 pounds), peeled and sliced into ⅜-inch-thick rounds

1 medium-size red bell pepper, diced

1 small onion, diced

12 small flour tortillas

4 cups shredded lettuce

2 medium-size to large ripe tomatoes, cut into thin wedges

2 ripe avocados, peeled, pitted, and sliced

Sour cream or grated Monterey Jack cheese

Homemade or store-bought salsa

1. Preheat the oven to 400°F. Lightly oil two rimmed baking sheets.

2. In a small bowl, combine the oil, cumin, garlic, and salt and pepper to taste. Brush both sides of the eggplant slices with the flavored oil and arrange in a single layer on the baking sheets. Scatter the bell pepper and onion on top.

3. Place the baking sheets side by side in the oven. Roast for 20 to 25 minutes, until the eggplant is well browned and very tender, turning once. (If the baking sheets do not fit side by side, place one on the middle rack and the other on the bottom rack and rotate them once or twice during the roasting process.) Remove from the oven and turn off the heat.

4. Wrap the tortillas in aluminum foil and place them in the warm oven for 10 to 15 minutes.

5. To serve, arrange the eggplant on one serving platter. Place the lettuce in the center of another serving platter. Surround the lettuce with the tomato wedges

and avocado slices. Pass the platters, warmed tortillas, sour cream, and salsa at the table and let the diners assemble their own fajitas.

Sandwich Heaven Sometimes it seems to me that the very best way to enjoy roasted vegetables is in a sandwich. Maybe roasted vegetables seem heaven-sent because vegetarian sandwiches are so limited compared to the wide range of fillings enjoyed by meat eaters. In fact, once you get beyond grilled cheese and frozen veggie burgers, the sandwich options become downright skimpy. Enter the roasted vegetable—which combines beautifully with pesto, coleslaw, tomato sauce, salsa, goat cheese, and relishes—and you have the start of an exquisite sandwich.

Barbecued Tempeh Sandwiches with Creamy Slaw

SERVES 5

IF ANYONE EVER STARTS a sandwich hall of fame, this delectable combination will surely place in the vegetarian category. The rich barbecue-flavored tempeh is sandwiched in a whole wheat bun with a mustardy coleslaw to make an unforgettable flavor experience.

CREAMY SLAW

6 cups finely grated green cabbage

2 medium-size carrots, finely grated

¼ cup minced onion

1 cup mayonnaise

2 tablespoons prepared yellow mustard

1 tablespoon dill pickle juice (brine from a bottle of dill pickles)

Salt and freshly ground black pepper

SANDWICHES

5 whole wheat kaiser rolls

Barbecue-Style Roasted Tempeh (page 205), warm or at room temperature

1. To make the slaw, combine the cabbage, carrots, onion, mayonnaise, mustard, and pickle juice in a large bowl. Mix well. Season with salt and pepper to taste and toss again. Let stand at room temperature for at least 30 minutes.

2. To assemble the sandwiches, slice open the rolls. Place about 4 tempeh slices on the bottom of each roll. Top with a generous dollop of coleslaw.

3. Serve at once, with plenty of napkins.

PLEASING PASTA

Linguine with Mixed Roasted Vegetables

Linguine with Roasted Ratatouille and Arugula

Fettuccine Alfredo with Roasted Vegetables

Creamy Penne and Roasted Vegetables

Orzo with Lemon-Roasted Summer Vegetables

Winter Vegetable Pasta with Goat Cheese

Marinated Artichoke and Mushroom Pasta

Bowties with Roasted Green Beans and Cheese

Orecchiette with Roasted Mushrooms

Saffron Pasta with Roasted Peppers

Baked Rigatoni with Roasted Zucchini and Eggplant

Ziti with Roasted Onions

Baked Orzo with Roasted Fennel and Red Peppers

Rich Vegetable Lasagna

White Lasagna with Roasted Vegetables

Linguine with Mixed Roasted Vegetables

SERVES 4

A SIMPLE DISH—quick to prepare and full of flavor. You can play with this recipe: change the vegetables, mellow the garlic by roasting it with the vegetables, substitute red wine vinegar for balsamic. A short pasta, such as rotini or penne, can replace the linguine. If you are feeding a particularly hungry crowd, you may want to use 1 pound pasta and increase the olive oil to ½ cup. When it comes to pasta and roasted vegetables, the combination works so well that the specifics can be altered without fear of ruining the recipe.

1 small to medium-size zucchini, cut into matchsticks

1 medium-size red bell pepper, cut into matchsticks

1 medium-size carrot, cut into matchsticks

1 small head radicchio, cut into matchsticks

4 canned or frozen and defrosted artichoke hearts, cut into matchsticks

1 shallot, sliced

6 tablespoons extra virgin olive oil

Salt and freshly ground black pepper

1 garlic clove, minced

2 tablespoons white (clear) balsamic vinegar, or more to taste

¼ cup chopped mixed fresh herb leaves, such as basil, mint, parsley, and chives

¾ pound linguine or fettuccine

½ cup freshly grated Parmesan cheese

½ cup chopped or sliced brine-cured black olives, such as Kalamata

1. Preheat the oven to 425°F. Lightly oil a large shallow roasting or half sheet pan.

2. In a large bowl, combine the zucchini, bell pepper, carrot, radicchio, artichokes, and shallot. Add 2 tablespoons of the oil and salt and pepper to taste. Toss to mix well. Arrange in a single layer in the pan. Do not wash the bowl.

3. Roast for 15 to 20 minutes, until the vegetables are lightly browned and tender, stirring or shaking the pan once or twice for even cooking.

4. Return the roasted vegetables to the bowl and toss with the garlic, vinegar, and herbs.

5. Meanwhile, cook the pasta in plenty of boiling salted water until *al dente*. Drain well.

6. Transfer the pasta to a large serving bowl and toss with the remaining 4 tablespoons oil and the cheese. Add the vegetables and olives and toss to mix well. Taste and adjust the seasonings, adding more salt, pepper, or vinegar as needed. Serve at once.

Linguine with Roasted Ratatouille and Arugula

SERVES 4 TO 6

A GENEROUS PLENTY of summer vegetables atop pasta—summer supper does not get much better than this. Serve with a green salad and French bread.

1 medium-size eggplant (about 1½ pounds), peeled and cut into ⅓-inch dice

1 medium-size zucchini, diced

1 medium-size yellow summer squash, diced

1 medium-size onion, diced

1 medium-size green bell pepper, diced

4 to 6 garlic cloves, thinly sliced

5 tablespoons extra virgin olive oil

2 tablespoons chopped fresh oregano leaves

Salt and freshly ground black pepper

1 pound linguine

1 cup freshly grated Parmesan cheese

One 14.5-ounce can diced tomatoes, with their juice

1 bunch (10 to 12 ounces) arugula or spinach, tough stems discarded and leaves torn

½ cup chopped brine-cured black olives, such as Kalamata, for garnish

1 tablespoon capers, drained, for garnish

1. Preheat the oven to 425°F. Lightly oil a large shallow roasting or half sheet pan.

2. In a large bowl, combine the eggplant, zucchini, summer squash, onion, bell pepper, and garlic. Add 3 tablespoons of the oil, the oregano, and salt and pepper to taste. Toss to coat. Arrange in a shallow (preferably single) layer in the pan.

3. Roast for 30 to 35 minutes, until the vegetables are lightly browned and tender, stirring or shaking the pan occasionally for even cooking.

4. Meanwhile, cook the pasta in plenty of boiling salted water until *al dente*. Drain well. Transfer to a large serving bowl. Add the remaining 2 tablespoons oil and the cheese and toss to mix. Keep warm.

5. In a medium-size saucepan, heat the tomatoes to boiling and remove from the heat. Stir in the roasted vegetables and arugula. Taste and adjust the seasonings, adding more salt and pepper as needed.

6. To serve, top the linguine with the vegetables and garnish with the olives and capers. Serve at once.

Fettuccine Alfredo with Roasted Vegetables

SERVES 4 TO 6

THE ORIGINAL *fettuccine all'Alfredo* was invented by a Roman restaurateur in 1914 to stimulate the appetite of his wife after she gave birth to their son. According to legend, Mary Pickford and Douglas Fairbanks enjoyed it on their honeymoon in Rome in 1927 and spread the fame of the dish, which I make somewhat less decadent with the addition of sweetly caramelized roasted vegetables.

2 small to medium-size zucchini, cut into matchsticks

1 small to medium-size yellow summer squash, cut into matchsticks

1 medium-size yellow bell pepper, cut into matchsticks

½ pound green beans, ends trimmed and cut into 1½-inch pieces

1 shallot, sliced

3 tablespoons extra virgin olive oil

Salt and freshly ground black pepper

1¼ pounds fresh fettuccine or 1 pound dried

1 cup freshly grated Parmesan cheese

1 garlic clove, minced

1½ cups half-and-half

10 fresh basil leaves, cut into thin ribbons, for garnish

1. Preheat the oven to 425°F. Lightly oil a large shallow roasting or half sheet pan.

2. In a large bowl, combine the zucchini, summer squash, bell pepper, green beans, and shallot. Add the oil and salt and pepper to taste. Toss to mix well. Arrange in a single layer in the pan.

3. Roast for 20 to 30 minutes, until the vegetables are lightly browned and tender, stirring once or twice for even cooking.

4. Meanwhile, cook the pasta in plenty of boiling salted water until *al dente*. Drain well.

5. Transfer the pasta to a large serving bowl and toss with the cheese and garlic. Add the half-and-half and toss again. Add the vegetables and toss to mix. Taste and adjust the seasonings, adding more salt and pepper as needed. Garnish with the basil and serve at once.

Creamy Penne and Roasted Vegetables

SERVES 4 TO 6

THERE IS NO LIMIT to the variations that can be created when pasta and roasted vegetables are combined. In this dish, ricotta is used to make an instant sauce. The timing of the steps works beautifully: while the pasta water heats, the vegetables roast. The hot pasta is tossed with ricotta, chopped tomatoes, and herbs. Then the roasted vegetables are added to make a wonderfully satisfying one-dish meal.

2 medium-size red bell peppers, cut into matchsticks

1 small to medium-size zucchini, cut into matchsticks

1 medium-size fennel bulb, cut into matchsticks and stalks discarded

½ pound mushrooms, trimmed and sliced

4 garlic cloves, minced

3 tablespoons extra virgin olive oil

Salt and freshly ground black pepper

1 pound penne, ziti, or other tubular pasta

1 pound (about 2 cups) ricotta cheese

1½ cups seeded and diced ripe tomatoes or one 14.5-ounce can diced tomatoes, drained

¼ cup chopped fresh basil leaves, or more to taste

¼ cup chopped fresh mint leaves, or more to taste

¼ cup chopped scallions, white and tender green parts only

1. Preheat the oven to 425°F. Lightly oil a large shallow roasting or half sheet pan.

2. In a large bowl, combine the bell peppers, zucchini, fennel, mushrooms, and garlic. Add the oil and salt and pepper to taste. Toss to mix well. Arrange in a single layer in the pan.

3. Roast for 20 to 25 minutes, until the vegetables are lightly browned and tender, stirring or shaking the pan occasionally for even cooking.

4. Meanwhile, cook the pasta in plenty of boiling salted water until *al dente*. Drain well.

5. Transfer the pasta to a large serving bowl and toss with the ricotta, tomatoes, basil, mint, and scallions. Add the vegetables and toss to mix. Taste and adjust the seasonings, adding more salt, pepper, or herbs as needed. Serve at once.

Orzo with Lemon-Roasted Summer Vegetables

SERVES 4 TO 6

A LIGHT, LIGHT DISH for summer, with plenty of fresh vegetables and bold flavors. This is a great recipe to make when you have a little of this and a little of that in the refrigerator—or ripening in the garden. Feel free to substitute other vegetables or increase the quantities and narrow the assortment.

Zest and juice of 1 lemon, or more juice to taste

2 garlic cloves, peeled but left whole

¼ cup chopped mixed fresh herb leaves, such as basil, mint, parsley, and chives

¼ cup plus 2 tablespoons extra virgin olive oil

Salt and freshly ground black pepper

1 small yellow summer squash, diced

1 medium-size red bell pepper, cut into matchsticks

1 medium-size carrot, cut into matchsticks

1 broccoli spear, stem peeled and diced and florets cut into 1-inch pieces

½ pound green beans, ends trimmed and cut into 1-inch pieces

1 pound orzo

½ cup high-quality neutral-tasting chicken or vegetable broth

½ cup freshly grated Parmesan cheese

1. Preheat the oven to 425°F. Lightly oil a large shallow roasting or half sheet pan.

2. In a food processor, finely mince the lemon zest, garlic, and herbs. Add the lemon juice and puree. With the motor running, slowly add the oil and process until it is fully incorporated. Pour the mixture into a glass measuring cup. Season with salt and pepper to taste.

3. In a large bowl, combine the summer squash, bell pepper, carrot, broccoli, and green beans. Pour half the lemon and oil mixture over the vegetables and toss to coat. Arrange in a single layer in the pan.

4. Roast for 15 to 20 minutes, until the vegetables are lightly browned and tender, stirring or shaking the pan once or twice for even cooking.

5. Meanwhile, cook the pasta in plenty of boiling salted water until *al dente*. Drain well.

6. Transfer the pasta to a serving bowl. Add the broth to the remaining lemon and oil mixture and whisk to combine. Pour over the pasta and toss to coat. Add the roasted vegetables and cheese. Toss to mix. Taste and adjust the seasonings, adding more salt, pepper, or lemon juice as needed. Serve at once.

Mushrooms Are Always an Option When you roast an assortment of mixed vegetables, it is always an option to substitute other vegetables for the ones called for in the recipe. Just be sure to cut all the vegetables the same size. I tend to avoid adding mushrooms to mixes of summer vegetables, as I find that they dominate delicately flavored vegetables. But if you are a mushroom lover, feel free to add them.

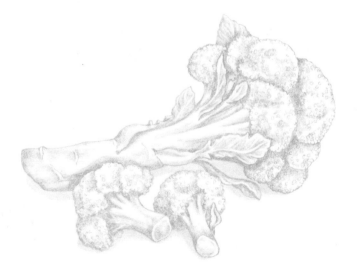

Winter Vegetable Pasta with Goat Cheese

SERVES 4 TO 6

ROASTED ROOT VEGETABLES and goat cheese are one of my favorite flavor combinations. Be sure to season generously with salt and pepper; otherwise, the flavor will be flat.

2 medium-size beets, peeled and cut into ½-inch dice

1 small butternut squash (about 1 pound), peeled, seeded, and cut into ½-inch dice

1 small rutabaga, peeled and cut into ½-inch dice

1 medium-size onion, halved and slivered

6 garlic cloves, thinly sliced

3 tablespoons extra virgin olive oil

1 teaspoon chopped fresh rosemary leaves

Salt and freshly ground black pepper

1 pound penne, ziti, or other tubular pasta

4 ounces mild fresh goat cheese, such as Montrachet

¼ cup dry white wine

1. Preheat the oven to 425°F. Lightly oil a large shallow roasting or half sheet pan.

2. In a large bowl, combine the beets, squash, rutabaga, onion, and garlic. Add the oil, rosemary, and salt and pepper to taste. Toss to coat well. Arrange in a single layer in the pan.

3. Roast for 35 to 45 minutes, until the vegetables are tender and lightly browned, stirring or shaking the pan occasionally for even cooking. Remove from the oven and keep warm.

4. Meanwhile, cook the pasta in plenty of boiling salted water until *al dente*. Drain well, reserving ½ cup of the cooking water. Transfer the pasta to a large serving bowl and keep warm.

5. In a small bowl, mash the cheese with a fork. Add the pasta cooking water and wine. Stir with the fork until creamy.

6. Toss the pasta with the cheese mixture. Top with the roasted vegetables and toss to mix. Season generously with salt and pepper. Serve at once.

Marinated Artichoke and Mushroom Pasta

SERVES 4 TO 6

BECAUSE YOU ARE STARTING with bottled marinated artichoke hearts, this recipe is quick to make. The combination of artichokes, mushrooms, and leeks is particularly luxurious for such a simple dish.

Four 6-ounce jars marinated artichoke hearts
¼ pound cremini mushrooms, trimmed and sliced
1 large leek, white part only, thinly sliced
6 garlic cloves, thinly sliced
1 pound linguine or spaghetti
1 tablespoon extra virgin olive oil
⅓ cup dry white wine
¼ cup chopped fresh basil leaves
Salt and freshly ground black pepper
Freshly grated Parmesan cheese

1. Preheat the oven to 425°F. Lightly oil a large shallow roasting or half sheet pan.

2. In a large bowl, combine the artichokes with marinade, mushrooms, leek, and garlic. Toss to coat with the marinade. Using a slotted spoon, transfer the vegetables to the pan and arrange in a single layer. Reserve the marinade in a small saucepan.

3. Roast for 15 to 20 minutes, until the vegetables are tender and lightly browned, stirring occasionally.

4. Meanwhile, cook the pasta in plenty of boiling salted water until *al dente*. Drain well. Transfer the pasta to a large serving bowl. Add the oil and toss well. Keep warm.

5. Add the wine to the marinade in the saucepan. Bring to a boil.

6. Add the vegetables, marinade mixture, and basil to the pasta. Season with salt and pepper to taste. Toss to mix.

7. Serve at once, passing the cheese at the table.

Bowties with Roasted Green Beans and Cheese

SERVES 4 TO 6

SIMPLICITY IS THE SIGNATURE of this quickly assembled pasta, which features roasted green beans in the starring role.

2 pounds green beans, ends trimmed and cut into 1½-inch pieces

2 garlic cloves, slivered

2 shallots, sliced

2 tablespoons extra virgin olive oil

Coarse sea salt or kosher salt

1 pound bowtie pasta

2 tablespoons butter

8 ounces (about 1 cup) ricotta cheese

¼ cup freshly grated Parmesan cheese

Salt and freshly ground black pepper

1. Preheat the oven to 450°F. Lightly oil two rimmed baking sheets.

2. Combine the green beans, garlic, shallots, and oil in a large bowl. Toss to coat well. Arrange in a single layer on the sheets.

3. Place the baking sheets side by side in the oven. Roast for about 15 minutes, until the beans are well browned, stirring or shaking the sheets occasionally for even cooking. (If the baking sheets do not fit side by side, place one on the middle rack and the other on the lower rack and rotate them occasionally during the roasting process.) Sprinkle lightly with the coarse salt.

4. Meanwhile, cook the pasta in plenty of boiling salted water until *al dente*. Drain well.

5. Transfer the pasta to a large serving bowl, add the butter, and toss. Add the ricotta and Parmesan and toss again. Add the green beans and season with salt to taste and plenty of pepper. Toss to mix well and serve at once.

Bowties with Roasted Asparagus and Ricotta: **Replace the green beans with 1 pound asparagus. Trim the asparagus and proceed with the recipe as above.**

Orecchiette with Roasted Mushrooms

BECAUSE MUSHROOMS CONTAIN so much water, they have a much greater volume when raw than when cooked. Sautéing mushrooms on top of the stove in quantity requires working in batches, but roasting them in a large pan solves the problem, and frees your attention for other tasks. This is a deliciously easy dish to prepare.

---

2 pounds mixed mushrooms, such as white button, shiitake, cremini, portobello, and oyster, trimmed and sliced

2 shallots, thinly sliced

2 garlic cloves, crushed

2 tablespoons chopped fresh sage leaves

¼ cup extra virgin olive oil

Coarse sea salt or kosher salt and freshly ground black pepper

1 pound orecchiette, cavatelli, or other cup-shaped pasta

1 bunch (10 to 12 ounces) fresh spinach, leaves torn and tough stems discarded

1 cup crème fraîche, half-and-half, or sour cream

¼ cup freshly grated Parmesan cheese

1. Preheat the oven to 450°F. Lightly oil a large shallow roasting or half sheet pan.

2. In a large bowl, combine the mushrooms, shallots, garlic, sage, and oil. Add salt and pepper to taste. Toss to coat well. Arrange in a single layer in the pan.

3. Roast for about 25 minutes, until the mushrooms are tender and well browned but not dry, stirring or shaking the pan occasionally for even cooking.

4. Meanwhile, cook the pasta in plenty of boiling salted water until *al dente*. Stir the spinach into the pot with the pasta, then drain well. The spinach will be just wilted.

5. Transfer the pasta and spinach to a large serving bowl. Add the crème fraîche and toss well. Add the mushrooms and cheese and toss again. Taste and adjust the seasonings. Serve at once.

Saffron Pasta with Roasted Peppers

SERVES 4 TO 6

THIS GOLDEN, RICH PASTA could define luxury. The sauce is made from a puree of roasted yellow bell peppers, scented with saffron, and made silky smooth with the addition of half-and-half.

4 yellow bell peppers

2 red bell peppers

2 garlic cloves, peeled but left whole

1 cup high-quality neutral-tasting chicken or vegetable broth

¼ cup dry white wine

Generous pinch of saffron threads, crumbled

1 cup half-and-half

1 pound linguine or rotini

¼ cup chopped fresh basil leaves

Salt and freshly ground black pepper

A few sprigs fresh basil, for garnish

1. Preheat the broiler. Lightly oil a rimmed baking sheet.

2. Place the bell peppers on the baking sheet with space between them. Broil 4 inches from the heat for 15 to 20 minutes, until charred all over, turning several times.

3. Place the peppers in a covered bowl, plastic bag, or paper bag. Seal and let steam for about 10 minutes to loosen the skins.

4. Cut slits in the peppers and drain briefly into a small bowl to catch any juices. Scrape or peel the skins and discard. Scrape and discard the seeds and membranes.

5. Chop the yellow peppers. Combine them in a food processor or blender with the garlic and pepper juices. Process until finely chopped. Add the broth and wine and process to make a smooth puree. Transfer to a saucepan and add the saffron and half-and-half. Heat gently over medium heat, stirring occasionally.

6. Cut the red peppers into thin, 1½-inch-long strips.

7. Cook the pasta in plenty of boiling salted water until *al dente*. Drain well.

8. Transfer the pasta to a large serving bowl. Add the saffron sauce, red pepper strips, and chopped basil. Toss to combine. Add salt and pepper to taste. Serve at once, garnished with the basil sprigs.

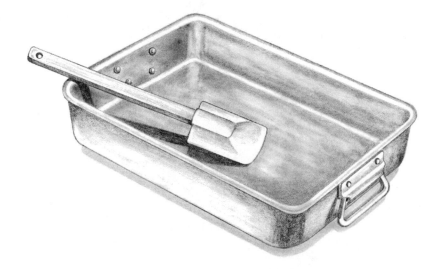

Baked Rigatoni with Roasted Zucchini and Eggplant

SERVES 4 TO 6

COULD YOU MAKE this dish by sautéing the vegetables rather than roasting them? Of course you could—but it would require more oil and more attention, and the flavor would be diminished. This is a great make-ahead dish—and it is very easy to throw together.

2 small to medium-size zucchini, quartered and sliced

1 large eggplant (1¾ to 2 pounds), peeled and cut into ⅓-inch dice

1 medium-size onion, thinly sliced

4 garlic cloves, thinly sliced

2 teaspoons chopped fresh oregano leaves

¼ cup extra virgin olive oil

Salt and freshly ground black pepper

1 pound rigatoni

One 28-ounce can peeled Italian tomatoes, with their juice

¼ cup torn fresh basil leaves

2 tablespoons chopped fresh mint leaves

8 ounces mozzarella cheese, shredded (about 2 cups)

1 cup freshly grated Parmesan cheese

1. Preheat the oven to 425°F. Lightly oil a large shallow roasting or half sheet pan.

2. In a large bowl, combine the zucchini, eggplant, onion, and garlic. Add the oregano, oil, and salt and pepper to taste. Toss to coat. Arrange in a shallow (preferably single) layer in the pan. Do not wash the bowl.

3. Roast for 25 to 35 minutes, until the vegetables are lightly browned and tender, stirring or shaking the pan occasionally for even cooking. Remove from the oven and reduce the temperature to 350°F.

4. Meanwhile, cook the pasta in plenty of boiling salted water until *al dente*. Drain well, reserving ¼ cup of the cooking water.

5. Pour the tomatoes with their juice into the bowl that held the vegetables. Using your hands, break up the tomatoes into small chunks. Add the roasted vegetables, pasta, reserved cooking water, basil, mint, and mozzarella.

6. Transfer the pasta mixture to a 9 x 13-inch baking dish. Sprinkle the Parmesan evenly over the top. (The casserole can be covered and held in the refrigerator for up to 6 hours. Adjust the baking time if it goes into the oven cold.)

7. Bake for 20 to 30 minutes, until heated through.

8. Serve hot.

Mix and Match I have never tasted a combination of roasted vegetables and pasta that I did not enjoy. Use these recipes as guidelines, but feel free to substitute different vegetables, different shapes of pasta, even different styles of sauce. Tomato, cream, cheese, pesto—they all combine harmoniously with pasta and roasted vegetables.

Ziti with Roasted Onions

SERVES 4 TO 6

THE SWEET CARAMELIZED ONIONS are perfectly balanced by the tangy Pecorino Romano cheese and dry wine. When you tire of the same old cream- or tomato-based pasta dishes, this makes a delicious change of pace.

6 cups thinly sliced onions (1½ pounds)

2 tablespoons butter, melted

2 tablespoons extra virgin olive oil

Salt and freshly ground black pepper

1 pound ziti, penne, or other tubular pasta

½ cup dry white wine

¼ cup chopped fresh parsley leaves

1 teaspoon chopped fresh rosemary leaves

½ cup freshly grated Pecorino Romano or Parmesan cheese

1. Preheat the oven to 425°F. Lightly oil a large shallow roasting or half sheet pan.

2. In a large bowl, combine the onions, butter, and oil. Season with salt and pepper to taste. Toss to mix well. Arrange in a shallow layer in the pan.

3. Roast for about 30 minutes, until the onions are golden and meltingly tender, stirring occasionally for even cooking.

4. Meanwhile, cook the pasta in plenty of boiling salted water until *al dente*. Drain well.

5. When the onions are tender, stir in the wine and return to the oven for another 5 minutes, until the wine is mostly evaporated.

6. Transfer the pasta to a large serving bowl. Add the onions, parsley, rosemary, and cheese and toss well. Taste and adjust the seasonings, being especially generous with the pepper. Serve hot.

Baked Orzo with Roasted Fennel and Red Peppers

SERVES 4 TO 6

SWEET FENNEL, COMBINED with salty, tangy feta cheese, olives, and capers, makes this a fragrant dish that holds up well—on a buffet table or in a covered dish held for late stragglers to dinner.

1 medium-size fennel bulb, cut into matchsticks, stalks discarded, and feathery leaves chopped

1 medium-size red bell pepper, cut into matchsticks

1 shallot, thinly sliced

1 garlic clove, minced

3 tablespoons extra virgin olive oil

Salt and freshly ground black pepper

1 pound orzo

2 medium-size ripe tomatoes, peeled, seeded, and chopped

4 ounces feta cheese, crumbled (about 1 cup)

¼ cup chopped brine-cured black olives, such as Kalamata

¼ cup chopped fresh parsley leaves

1 tablespoon capers, drained

1. Preheat the oven to 425°F.

2. Combine the fennel bulb, bell pepper, shallot, and garlic in a 9 x 13-inch baking dish. Add 2 tablespoons of the oil and toss to coat. Season with salt and pepper to taste. Arrange in a shallow layer.

3. Roast for 15 to 20 minutes, until the vegetables are lightly browned and tender, stirring once or twice for even cooking. Remove from the oven and reduce the temperature to 350°F.

4. Meanwhile, cook the orzo in boiling salted water until *al dente*. Drain well.

5. Add the orzo and remaining 1 tablespoon oil to the baking dish and toss to coat. Add the tomatoes, cheese, olives, parsley, capers, and 1 tablespoon of the chopped fennel leaves. Toss together. Taste and adjust the seasonings. Cover tightly with aluminum foil.

6. Bake for 20 to 30 minutes, until the cheese is melted.

7. Serve hot.

Rich Vegetable Lasagna

SERVES 6 TO 9

THIS RICH-TASTING LASAGNA bears only a passing resemblance to the watery spinach lasagna that is a common alternative to meat lasagna. Roasted vegetables add flavor and texture to the traditional tomato sauce.

1 small to medium-size eggplant (1 to 1½ pounds), peeled and cut into ⅓-inch dice

1 medium-size zucchini, cut into ⅓-inch dice

1 medium-size red or green bell pepper, cut into ⅓-inch dice

1 medium-size onion, cut into ⅓-inch dice

½ pound mushrooms, trimmed and chopped

¼ cup extra virgin olive oil

4 garlic cloves, thinly sliced

2 teaspoons chopped fresh rosemary leaves

2 teaspoons chopped fresh thyme leaves

Salt and freshly ground black pepper

6 cups well-seasoned tomato sauce, homemade (page 62) or store-bought

1 pound (about 2 cups) ricotta cheese

1 large egg, lightly beaten

2 tablespoons chopped fresh basil leaves

12 no-cook lasagna noodles

1 pound mozzarella cheese, shredded (about 4 cups)

1 cup freshly grated Parmesan cheese

1. Preheat the oven to 425°F. Lightly oil a large shallow roasting or half sheet pan.

2. In a large bowl, combine the eggplant, zucchini, bell pepper, onion, and mushrooms. Add the oil, garlic, rosemary, thyme, and salt and pepper to taste. Toss to coat. Arrange in a shallow (preferably single) layer in the pan. Do not wash the bowl.

3. Roast for 35 to 40 minutes, until the vegetables are tender and well browned, stirring occasionally for even cooking. Remove from the oven and reduce the temperature to 350°F.

4. In the large bowl, combine the roasted vegetables and tomato sauce. You should have approximately 10 cups of vegetable sauce. Taste and adjust the seasonings.

5. Combine the ricotta, egg, and basil in a medium-size bowl and mix well.

6. To assemble the lasagna, spread about 2 cups of the sauce in a 9 x 13-inch baking dish. Place 3 lasagna noodles over the sauce. The noodles should not touch or overlap. Spread one-third of the ricotta mixture evenly over the noodles. Top with another 1½ to 2 cups sauce. Sprinkle one-quarter of the mozzarella and one-quarter of the Parmesan on top. Repeat the layers two more times. Top with the remaining 3 lasagna noodles. Spread the remaining sauce on top and sprinkle with the remaining cheeses. Cover with aluminum foil.

7. Bake for 30 minutes. Remove the foil and bake for another 10 to 15 minutes, until hot and bubbly.

8. Let stand for 5 minutes before cutting.

9. Serve hot or warm.

Make-Ahead Notes The lasagna can be assembled and held for up to 8 hours in the refrigerator. Add 15 minutes to the baking time if the lasagna is cold when placed in the oven. The lasagna also can be baked in advance and frozen for up to 1 month. Bake it still frozen and covered with foil, adding 30 minutes to the baking time.

White Lasagna with Roasted Vegetables

SERVES 6 TO 9

FENNEL IS THE FEATURED performer in this subtle lasagna. Where nutmeg might be expected in the white sauce, chopped fennel leaves add an unexpectedly fresh flair. The eggplant plays the supporting role of "meat," while the red bell peppers add color. This is a dish that can be made in advance and baked just prior to serving. It retains its architectural integrity when served (it does not slide apart), so it makes a lovely-looking dinner accompanied by a salad of lightly dressed greens.

2 medium-size red bell peppers, diced

1 medium-size eggplant (about 1½ pounds), peeled and cut into ⅓-inch dice

1 large fennel bulb, diced, stalks discarded, and feathery leaves chopped and reserved

1 medium-size leek, white and tender green parts only, thinly sliced

3 tablespoons extra virgin olive oil

Salt and freshly ground black pepper

12 lasagna noodles

6 tablespoons (¾ stick) butter

3 garlic cloves, minced

6 tablespoons unbleached all-purpose flour

2 ¾ cups milk

½ cup dry white wine

Salt and freshly ground black pepper

2 cups freshly grated Parmesan cheese

1. Preheat the oven to 425°F. Lightly oil a large shallow roasting or half sheet pan.

2. In a large bowl, combine the bell peppers, eggplant, fennel bulb, and leek. Add the oil and salt and pepper to taste. Toss to coat. Arrange in a shallow (preferably single) layer in the pan.

3. Roast for 25 to 35 minutes, until the vegetables are lightly browned and tender, stirring or shaking the pan occasionally for even cooking.

4. Meanwhile, cook the lasagna noodles in plenty of boiling salted water until *al dente*. Drain, rinse, and set aside.

5. To prepare the sauce, melt the butter in a medium-size heavy-bottomed saucepan over medium heat. Add the garlic and sauté until fragrant, about

2 minutes. Whisk in the flour to make a smooth paste. Cook, whisking constantly, for 1 minute. Add the milk and whisk until smooth. Bring to a slow boil and stir in the wine and 2 tablespoons of the chopped fennel leaves. Season with salt and pepper and more fennel leaves, if desired. Remove from the heat.

6. When the vegetables are done, remove from the oven and reduce the temperature to 350°F.

7. To assemble the lasagna, spread about ½ cup of the sauce in a 9 x 13-inch baking dish. Place 3 lasagna noodles on top. Pour about ½ cup of the sauce evenly over the noodles. Spread about one-third of the roasted vegetables evenly over the sauce. Sprinkle about one-quarter of the Parmesan on top. Repeat the layers two more times. Top with the remaining 3 lasagna noodles. Spread the remaining sauce on top and sprinkle with the remaining Parmesan. Cover with aluminum foil. (The lasagna can be assembled and held for up to 8 hours in the refrigerator. Add 10 minutes to the baking time if it is cold when placed in the oven.)

8. Bake for 30 minutes. Remove the foil and bake for another 10 to 15 minutes, until hot and bubbly.

9. Let stand for 5 minutes before cutting.

10. Serve hot or warm.

TEMPTING TARTS, PASTRIES, AND PIZZAS

Fall Vegetable Tart

THIS RUSTIC VEGETABLE TART is one of my favorites, and I make it often—with whatever cheese I happen to have on hand. Fontina is my favorite (the version here), with soft goat cheese (crumbled rather than grated) a close contender. Gruyère and cheddar both work, although I find their flavors a little too assertive against the sweet roasted vegetables. This is a very adaptable tart, however, so feel free to experiment with different cheeses and different vegetables. Then add a green salad for a delicious light meal.

---

2 medium-size beets, peeled and cut into ⅓-inch dice

1 small butternut squash (about 1 pound), peeled, seeded, and cut into ⅓-inch dice

1 medium-size onion, halved and slivered

1 medium-size red bell pepper, diced

2 cups sliced mushrooms

6 garlic cloves, thinly sliced

2 tablespoons extra virgin olive oil

1 teaspoon chopped fresh rosemary leaves

Salt and freshly ground black pepper

Homemade or store-bought pastry for one 9- or 10-inch pie

8 ounces fontina cheese, grated (about 2 cups)

1. Preheat the oven to 425°F. Lightly oil a large shallow roasting or half sheet pan.

2. In a large bowl, combine the beets, squash, onion, bell pepper, mushrooms, and garlic. Add the oil, rosemary, and salt and pepper to taste. Toss to coat well. Arrange in a shallow (preferably single) layer in the pan.

3. Roast for 35 to 45 minutes, until the vegetables are tender and lightly browned, stirring or shaking the pan occasionally for even cooking. Remove from the oven and reduce the temperature to 375°F.

4. Line a baking sheet with aluminum foil. Place the pastry on the baking sheet. Unfold the pastry and pinch together any tears. Sprinkle the cheese over the pastry, leaving a 2-inch border around the edge. Arrange the roasted vegetables on top of the cheese. Fold the dough up to partially cover the filling and crimp to seal the edges.

5. Bake for about 25 minutes, until the crust is golden.

6. Cut into wedges and serve warm.

A Better Tart Shell Normally I don't like store-bought convenience foods, but I make an exception where pastry is concerned. Look for Pillsbury prepared pie crusts in the refrigerated section of your supermarket. Inside the red box are two folded sheets of pastry. The pastry is incredibly easy to handle and the resulting crust is tender, flaky, and buttery. However, you can make your own tart shell, using your favorite recipe for a 9- or 10-inch pie or tart crust.

Roasted Vegetable Quiche

A TERRIFIC BRUNCH OPTION. This quiche is a great make-ahead dish. You can even roast the vegetables the day before you prepare the quiche.

Homemade or store-bought pastry for one 9- or 10-inch pie

1 medium-size red bell pepper, diced

½ pound mushrooms, trimmed and sliced

½ pound green beans or asparagus, ends or bottoms trimmed and cut into 1-inch pieces

1 shallot, finely chopped

2 tablespoons extra virgin olive oil

1 teaspoon chopped fresh or dried rosemary

Salt and freshly ground black pepper

2 large eggs, well beaten

About 1 cup half-and-half or whole milk

4 ounces Gruyère cheese, grated (about 1 cup)

1. Fit the pastry into a 9- or 10-inch quiche dish or pie plate. Trim and crimp the edge. Set aside in the refrigerator while you prepare the filling.

2. Preheat the oven to 425°F. Lightly oil a large shallow roasting or half sheet pan.

3. In a large bowl, combine the bell pepper, mushrooms, green beans, and shallot. Add the oil, rosemary, and salt and pepper to taste. Toss to coat well. Arrange in a shallow (preferably single) layer in the pan.

4. Roast for 25 to 30 minutes, until the vegetables are tender and lightly browned, stirring or shaking the pan occasionally for even cooking. Remove from the oven and reduce the temperature to 375°F.

5. Combine the eggs with enough half-and-half to make 1½ cups. Season with salt and pepper. Whisk until completely blended. Sprinkle the cheese in the crust. Cover with the vegetables. Pour the egg mixture over all.

6. Bake for 25 to 35 minutes, until the filling is set. Let rest for at least 10 minutes.

7. Cut into wedges and serve warm or at room temperature.

Onion Tart Niçoise

SERVES 4 TO 6

THIS TRADITIONAL ONION TART from Nice is called a *pissaladière* and takes its name from the anchovy paste, *pissala*, that is often brushed on the tart. It is similar to a pizza but is made without cheese. Unlike pizza, it is best served as an appetizer, although it can hold its own on a buffet table with several pizza choices. This vegetarian version skips the anchovies, but if you like them, arrange about 12 anchovy fillets in a latticework pattern over the onions, with an olive placed inside each of the resulting diamonds.

½ recipe Basic Pizza Dough (page 200)
4 large onions, thinly sliced
6 garlic cloves, thinly sliced
3 tablespoons extra virgin olive oil
2 tablespoons chopped fresh thyme leaves
Salt and freshly ground black pepper
1 cup brine-cured black olives, such as Kalamata

1. Prepare the pizza dough and set aside in a warm, draft-free place to rise for about 1 hour, until doubled in bulk.

2. Preheat the oven to 425°F. Lightly oil a large roasting pan or half sheet pan.

3. In a large bowl, combine the onions, garlic, oil, thyme, and salt and pepper to taste. Toss to coat. Arrange in a shallow (preferably single) layer in the pan.

4. Roast for 30 minutes, until the onions are golden and meltingly tender, stirring occasionally for even cooking. Remove from the oven and increase the temperature to 500°F.

5. Lightly oil a 10- or 12-inch round pizza pan or a 12 x 15-inch baking sheet. Stretch the dough to fit the pan. Spread the onions over the dough. Scatter the olives over the onions.

6. Bake the tart on the bottom rack for 12 to 15 minutes, until the crust is golden.

7. Cut into wedges or rectangles and serve warm.

Parmesan Tart with Roasted Tomatoes and Fennel

SERVES 4 TO 6

THE SWEETNESS OF fennel and tomatoes is nicely balanced by the tang of Parmesan. This is an elegant yet simple tart that can be served as a main course or as a starter for a more formal meal.

18 ripe plum tomatoes, halved and cored

4 garlic cloves, sliced

4 tablespoons extra virgin olive oil

Salt and freshly ground black pepper

2 fennel bulbs, cut into matchsticks and stalks discarded

Homemade or store-bought pastry for one 9- or 10-inch pie

1 cup freshly grated Parmesan cheese

3 tablespoons finely chopped fresh parsley leaves

¼ cup fine dry bread crumbs

1. Preheat the oven to 400°F. Lightly oil two 9 x 13-inch baking dishes.

2. Arrange the tomato halves cut side down in a single layer in one of the baking dishes.

3. Roast for 30 minutes, until the tomatoes are beginning to brown. Remove from the oven but leave the oven on. Lift the skins off the tomatoes and discard; they should separate easily from the flesh. Add the garlic and drizzle 2 tablespoons of the oil over the tomatoes. Season with salt and pepper to taste.

4. Meanwhile, arrange the fennel in a shallow layer in the second baking dish. Drizzle with the remaining 2 tablespoons oil, season with salt and pepper to taste, and toss to coat.

5. Place the baking dishes side by side in the oven. Roast for about 30 minutes, until the fennel is tender and lightly browned, stirring occasionally for even cooking. (If the baking dishes do not fit side by side, place one on the middle rack and the other on the bottom rack and rotate them once or twice during the roasting process.)

6. When the tomatoes and fennel are done, remove from the oven and reduce the temperature to 375°F.

7. Fit the pastry into a 9- or 10-inch quiche dish or pie plate. Trim and crimp the edge. Sprinkle ½ cup of the Parmesan over the crust. Cover the Parmesan with the tomatoes and garlic and sprinkle with the parsley. Cover the tomatoes with the fennel.

8. In a small bowl, combine the remaining ½ cup Parmesan and the bread crumbs. Taste and add salt and pepper, if needed. Sprinkle over the top of the tart.

9. Bake for about 30 minutes, until the crust and topping are golden.

10. Let the tart rest for at least 10 minutes.

11. Cut into wedges and serve warm or at room temperature.

Mediterranean Roasted Vegetable Pie

PHYLLO DOUGH IS incredibly easy to handle and yields impressive results. This pie is simple to make for a casual supper but worthy of company. The filling is a rich mélange of eggplant, zucchini, tomatoes, and feta cheese. A green salad and a steamed vegetable make the perfect accompaniments. And if you don't have any phyllo on hand? Make the filling and stuff it into pita pockets or a hollowed-out baguette. Or toss it with pasta, spoon it onto rice, or spread it on a pizza shell. These vegetables are delicious any way you serve them.

18 ripe plum tomatoes, halved and cored

1 medium-size to large eggplant (1½ to 2 pounds), peeled and cut into ⅓-inch dice

1 medium-size zucchini, cut into ⅓-inch dice

1 medium-size onion, halved and thinly sliced

¼ cup plus 1 tablespoon extra virgin olive oil

Salt and freshly ground black pepper

3 garlic cloves, minced

2 tablespoons chopped fresh parsley leaves

1 tablespoon chopped fresh oregano leaves

8 ounces feta cheese, crumbled (about 2 cups)

1 tablespoon sherry vinegar (optional)

3 tablespoons butter, melted

6 sheets phyllo dough (about 14 x 18 inches each), defrosted if frozen

1. Preheat the oven to 400°F. Lightly oil a 9 x 13-inch baking dish and a large shallow roasting pan or half sheet pan.

2. Arrange the tomato halves cut side down in a single layer in the baking dish. Roast for about 30 minutes, until the tomatoes are completely tender and beginning to brown.

3. Meanwhile, combine the eggplant, zucchini, and onion in a large bowl. Add ¼ cup of the oil and toss to coat. Season with salt and pepper to taste. Arrange in a shallow (preferably single) layer in the pan. Do not wash the bowl.

4. Place the roasting pan in the oven alongside the tomatoes. Roast for about 30 minutes, until the vegetables are completely tender and beginning to brown,

stirring every 10 minutes or so for even cooking. (If the pan and dish do not fit side by side, place the tomatoes on the middle rack and the mixed vegetables on the bottom rack and rotate them once or twice during the roasting process.) Remove from the oven and reduce the temperature to 375°F.

5. Lift the skins off the tomatoes and discard; they should separate easily from the flesh. Combine the other vegetables and the tomatoes in the large bowl. Add the garlic, parsley, and oregano. Toss to mix. Gently mix in the cheese. Season with salt and pepper to taste, adding the vinegar, if needed, to balance the sweetness of the tomatoes.

6. Combine the butter and remaining 1 tablespoon oil. Brush some of the butter mixture along the bottom and side of a deep-dish 9- or 10-inch pie plate. Fit 1 sheet of phyllo in the pie plate, allowing it to hang over the edge. Brush with some of the butter mixture. Top with 4 more sheets of phyllo, brushing each with the butter mixture before placing another sheet on top. Spoon the vegetable and cheese mixture into the pie plate. Fold the ends of the phyllo over the filling, brushing the pieces with the butter mixture as you do so. Cut the final sheet of phyllo to fit on top of the pie. Tuck the ends inside the pie plate and brush with more butter. With a sharp serrated knife, cut the pie into wedges, slicing through the top phyllo sheets only; do not cut through to the bottom layer.

7. Bake for about 30 minutes, until the crust is golden brown.

8. Let the pie rest for 5 to 10 minutes.

9. Cut into wedges and serve warm.

Winter Vegetable Strudel on a Bed of Greens

SERVES 4

MORE FUN WITH PHYLLO—this time a strudel filled with a sweet mix of roasted winter vegetables bound together with creamy goat cheese. To serve it as a main course, I place the still-warm strudel on a bed of lightly dressed greens. Some crusty French bread finishes the meal. You also can serve this strudel as an appetizer or hors d'oeuvre without the salad.

STRUDEL

1 fennel bulb, diced, stalks discarded, and feathery leaves chopped

1 large beet, peeled and cut into ⅓-inch dice

1 delicata squash or ½ pound butternut squash, peeled, seeded, and cut into ⅓-inch dice

1 medium-size leek, white part only, thinly sliced

4 tablespoons extra virgin olive oil

Salt and freshly ground black pepper

8 ounces mild fresh goat cheese, such as Montrachet, at room temperature, crumbled (about 2 cups)

¼ cup (½ stick) butter, melted

12 sheets phyllo dough (about 14 x 18 inches each), defrosted if frozen

SALAD

2 tablespoons white (clear) balsamic vinegar

½ teaspoon sugar

1 tablespoon extra virgin olive oil

Salt and freshly ground black pepper

8 to 10 cups torn mixed salad greens or mesclun, including some bitter or strong-tasting greens such as frisée, escarole, or watercress

1. Preheat the oven to 425°F. Lightly oil a large shallow roasting or half sheet pan.

2. In a large bowl, combine the fennel bulb, beet, squash, and leek. Add 2 tablespoons of the oil and salt and pepper to taste. Toss to coat. Arrange in a shallow (preferably single) layer in the pan. Do not wash the bowl.

3. Roast for about 25 minutes, until the vegetables are lightly browned and tender, stirring or shaking the pan occasionally for even cooking. Remove from the oven and reduce the temperature to 375°F.

4. Return the vegetables to the bowl and mix in the fennel leaves. As lightly as possible, mix in the goat cheese. If you mix too vigorously, the beets will stain the cheese and vegetables a lurid pink (which is okay for Valentine's Day), so it is preferable to mix lightly and leave the goat cheese in small chunks.

5. In a small bowl, combine the remaining 2 tablespoons oil and butter.

6. Open 1 sheet of the phyllo on a work surface. Brush with some of the butter mixture. Top with 5 more sheets of phyllo, brushing each with the butter mixture before placing another sheet on top. Spoon half the filling along the short end of the phyllo, leaving a border of about 1½ inches on each end. Fold the long sides in to enclose the filling. Roll the phyllo and filling over onto itself to form a roll. Place seam side down on a baking sheet. Brush with more of the butter mixture. Repeat with the remaining phyllo sheets and filling to make a second strudel.

7. Bake for about 25 minutes, until the strudels are golden brown.

8. Meanwhile, make the salad. In a small bowl, whisk together the vinegar and sugar. Gradually drizzle in the oil, whisking until emulsified. Season with salt and pepper to taste. Place the greens in a large salad bowl.

9. When the strudels are done, add the dressing to the salad and toss to mix. Divide the salad among four plates. Cut each strudel into 8 slices. Arrange 4 slices of strudel on each plate on top of the salad. Serve at once.

Tips for Handling Phyllo Phyllo is one of the easiest pastry doughs to work with. Here are some tips to guarantee your success.

- Look for phyllo in the frozen food section of your supermarket. You will get the best results buying the pastry from a market that turns over its stock regularly, as the dough does dry out over time.

- Store phyllo in the freezer for up to 2 months or in the refrigerator for up to 1 week. Phyllo dough can be frozen, defrosted, and refrozen without a significant loss of quality.

- Defrost frozen phyllo in the box at room temperature for about 5 hours.

- When working with phyllo, prepare all your other ingredients before you open the box.

- Work on a clean, dry surface.

- Work with one sheet of phyllo at a time. Keep the remaining phyllo covered with plastic wrap, then a damp towel. Do not leave the phyllo uncovered for more than a few minutes.
- Brush each sheet of phyllo with butter or oil. To lighten a dish, spray the phyllo with a mist of cooking oil or nonstick cooking spray instead. When brushing, work from the edges to the center to prevent the edges from cracking.
- Reroll any unused phyllo in plastic and seal tightly. Refrigerate or refreeze.

Veggie Pizza

SERVES 6

WHILE THE DOUGH rises, the vegetables roast—perfect timing for a vegetarian feast. This is a rather conventional pizza—with tomato sauce, mozzarella cheese, and vegetables.

1 recipe Basic Pizza Dough (page 200)
2 medium-size zucchini, cut into ⅓-inch dice
1 medium-size onion, cut into ⅓-inch dice
1 medium-size red or green bell pepper, cut into ⅓-inch dice
½ pound eggplant (½ small), peeled (optional) and cut into ⅓-inch dice
½ pound mushrooms, trimmed and chopped
3 tablespoons extra virgin olive oil
4 garlic cloves, minced
½ teaspoon dried rosemary, or more to taste
½ teaspoon dried thyme, or more to taste
Salt and freshly ground black pepper
3 cups well-seasoned tomato sauce, homemade (page 62), or store-bought
1 pound fresh mozzarella cheese, sliced

1. Prepare the pizza dough and set aside in a warm, draft-free place to rise for about 1 hour, until doubled in bulk.

2. Preheat the oven to 425°F. Lightly oil a large shallow roasting or half sheet pan.

3. In a large bowl, combine the zucchini, onion, bell pepper, eggplant, and mushrooms. Add the oil, garlic, rosemary, thyme, and salt and pepper to taste. Toss to coat. Arrange in a shallow (preferably single) layer in the pan.

4. Roast for 30 to 45 minutes, until the vegetables are well browned and tender, stirring or shaking the pan occasionally for even cooking. Remove from the oven and increase the temperature to 500°F.

5. Divide the dough into two balls. Lightly oil two 10- or 12-inch round pizza pans or two 12 x 15-inch baking sheets. Assemble and bake the pizzas one at a time. Stretch one ball of dough to fit one pan. Spoon half the tomato sauce over the dough. Scatter half the vegetables on the sauce and top with about half the mozzarella.

6. Bake on the bottom rack for 10 to 12 minutes, until the crust is golden.

7. Meanwhile, assemble the second pizza. Bake when the first pizza is done.

8. Serve both pizzas warm.

Mushroom-Pesto Pizza

SERVES 6

THIS PIZZA IS TOPPED with an intensely flavored paste of roasted mushrooms and walnuts, plus fresh tomatoes and mozzarella, resulting in a wonderful contrast of fresh and roasted flavors.

1 recipe Basic Pizza Dough (page 200)
1 pound mushrooms, trimmed and halved
¼ cup extra virgin olive oil
Salt and freshly ground black pepper
½ cup walnut pieces
4 garlic cloves, peeled but left whole
1 cup fresh basil leaves
½ cup freshly grated Parmesan cheese
2 large ripe tomatoes, thinly sliced
1 pound fresh mozzarella cheese, thinly sliced

1. Prepare the pizza dough and set aside in a warm, draft-free place to rise for about 1 hour, until doubled in bulk.

2. Preheat the oven to 425°F. Lightly oil a large shallow roasting or half sheet pan.

3. In a large bowl, toss the mushrooms with the oil and salt and pepper to taste. Arrange in a single layer in the pan.

4. Roast for about 15 minutes, until the mushrooms are well browned and juicy, stirring once or twice. Add the walnuts and roast for about another 7 minutes, until the mushrooms are browned and juicy and the walnuts are fragrant and beginning to color. Remove from the oven and increase the temperature to 500°F. Let the mushrooms cool briefly.

5. Combine the mushroom and walnut mixture, garlic, basil, and Parmesan in a food processor and pulse until finely chopped and blended. Do not puree; there should still be some texture to the pesto. Season to taste with salt and plenty of pepper.

6. Divide the dough into two balls. Lightly oil two 10- or 12-inch round pizza pans or two 12 x 15-inch baking sheets. Assemble and bake the pizzas one at a time. Stretch one ball of dough to fit one pan. Spread half the mushroom pesto

over the dough. Arrange half the tomatoes on the pesto and top with half the mozzarella.

7. Bake on the bottom rack for 10 to 12 minutes, until the crust is golden.

8. Meanwhile, assemble the second pizza. Bake when the first pizza is done.

9. Serve both pizzas warm.

Artichoke and Leek Stuffed Pizza

SERVES 6

WHY STUFF A PIZZA? When you want to emphasize the filling above the other components, a stuffed pizza is perfect. Roasted artichokes and leeks folded into a creamy, garlicky ricotta cheese mixture make the filling memorable. Plus, this impressive-looking pizza holds up well on a buffet table and transports easily to a potluck.

1 recipe Basic Pizza Dough (page 200)

8 canned or frozen and defrosted artichoke hearts, quartered

2 medium-size leeks, white and tender green parts only, sliced

1 medium-size zucchini, cut into matchsticks

1 medium-size red bell pepper, cut into matchsticks

4 tablespoons extra virgin olive oil

Salt and freshly ground black pepper

1 pound (about 2 cups) ricotta cheese

2 large eggs, lightly beaten

8 ounces mozzarella cheese, grated (about 2 cups)

½ cup freshly grated Parmesan cheese

½ cup coarsely chopped fresh basil leaves

3 garlic cloves, minced

1. Prepare the dough and set aside in a warm, draft-free place to rise for about 1 hour, until doubled in bulk.

2. Preheat the oven to 425°F. Lightly oil a large shallow roasting or half sheet pan.

3. In a large bowl, combine the artichokes, leeks, zucchini, and bell pepper. Add 3 tablespoons of the oil and salt and pepper to taste. Toss to coat. Arrange in a shallow (preferably single) layer in the pan. Do not wash the bowl.

4. Roast for about 30 minutes, until the vegetables are tender and lightly browned, stirring or shaking the pan occasionally for even cooking.

5. While the vegetables roast, combine the ricotta and eggs in the large bowl and mix. Add the mozzarella, ¼ cup of the Parmesan, the basil, and garlic. Mix well.

6. When the vegetables are done, remove from the oven and increase the temperature to 500°F. Add the roasted vegetables to the cheese mixture and mix well. Taste and adjust the seasonings.

7. Lightly oil a 14-inch round pizza pan. Divide the dough into two balls. Stretch one ball to fit the pan. Spread the filling over the dough, leaving a ⅛-inch border around the edge. Stretch the other ball of dough to make a circle about 14 inches in diameter and place it over the filling. Pinch together the top and bottom crusts. Brush with the remaining 1 tablespoon oil and sprinkle with the remaining ¼ cup Parmesan.

8. Bake on the middle rack for about 15 minutes, until the crust is golden.

9. Let the pizza stand for at least 10 minutes.

10. Cut into wedges and serve warm or at room temperature.

White Pizza with Roasted Winter Vegetables

SERVES 6

OF ALL THE pizza recipes in this chapter, this one is the richest. I make this pizza one at a time and cut the pieces small.

½ recipe Basic Pizza Dough (page 200)
1 medium-size fennel bulb, diced and stalks discarded
1 medium-size red bell pepper, diced
1 pound butternut or delicata squash, peeled, seeded, and diced
2 tablespoons extra virgin olive oil
1 teaspoon crumbled dried rosemary
Salt and freshly ground black pepper
3 garlic cloves, minced
1 pound (about 2 cups) ricotta cheese
½ cup freshly grated Parmesan cheese

1. Prepare the pizza dough and set aside in a warm, draft-free place to rise for about 1 hour, until doubled in bulk.

2. Preheat the oven to 425°F. Lightly oil a large shallow roasting or half sheet pan.

3. In a large bowl, combine the fennel, bell pepper, and squash. Add the oil, rosemary, and salt and pepper to taste. Toss to coat. Arrange in a shallow (preferably single) layer in the pan.

4. Roast for about 30 minutes, until the vegetables are well browned and tender, stirring or shaking the pan occasionally for even cooking. Remove from the oven and increase the temperature to 500°F.

5. Lightly oil a 10- or 12-inch round pizza pan or a 12 x 15-inch baking sheet. Stretch the dough to fit the pan.

6. Stir the garlic into the ricotta. Spread the ricotta over the dough. Scatter the vegetables on the ricotta and top with the Parmesan.

7. Bake on the bottom rack for 10 to 12 minutes, until the crust is golden and the Parmesan is melted.

8. Slice and serve warm.

Pesto Pizza with Roasted Vegetables

SERVES 6

IT IS FORTUNATE for those of us who live up north that pesto freezes so well. During the dog days of August, it is my custom to make pesto as frequently as my basil plants will allow and to freeze the extra in small plastic containers. The concentrated basil flavor of pesto is a fine match for the concentrated flavors of roasted vegetables.

1 recipe Basic Pizza Dough (page 200)
2 medium-size zucchini, cut into matchsticks
2 medium-size red bell peppers, cut into matchsticks
¼ pound mushrooms, trimmed and sliced
3 tablespoons extra virgin olive oil
2 garlic cloves, minced
Salt and freshly ground black pepper
2 cups pesto, homemade (page 104) or store-bought
1 pound fresh mozzarella cheese, sliced

1. Prepare the pizza dough and set aside in a warm, draft-free place to rise for about 1 hour, until doubled in bulk.

2. Meanwhile, preheat the oven to 425°F. Lightly oil a large shallow roasting pan or half sheet pan.

3. In a large bowl, combine the zucchini, bell peppers, and mushrooms. Add the oil, garlic, and salt and pepper to taste. Toss to coat. Arrange in a shallow (preferably single) layer in the pan.

4. Roast for 30 to 45 minutes, until the vegetables are well browned and tender, stirring or shaking the pan occasionally for even cooking. Remove from the oven and increase the temperature to 500°F.

5. Divide the dough into two balls. Lightly oil two 10- or 12-inch round pizza pans or two 12 x 15-inch baking sheets. Assemble and bake the pizzas one at a time. Stretch one ball of dough to fit one pan. Spread half the pesto over the dough. Scatter half the vegetables on the pesto and top with about half the mozzarella.

6. Bake on the bottom rack for 10 to 12 minutes, until the crust is golden.

7. Meanwhile, assemble the second pizza. Bake when the first pizza is done.

8. Serve both pizzas warm.

Basic Pizza Dough

3¾ to 4 cups unbleached all-purpose flour
1 tablespoon salt
1½ cups warm (110° to 115°F) water
One ¼-ounce packet or 1 tablespoon active dry yeast
3 tablespoons olive oil

1. In a food processor fitted with a dough hook or in a large bowl, combine the flour and salt. Measure the warm water into a glass measure, add the yeast, and stir until foamy. Stir in the oil.

2. Pour the water mixture into the food processor with the motor running and process until the dough forms into a ball. Continue processing for 1 minute to knead the dough. Alternatively, add the yeast mixture to the bowl and stir until the dough comes together into a ball. Turn out onto a lightly floured surface and knead until the dough is springy and elastic, about 5 minutes. The dough should be firm and just slightly sticky—not dry.

3. Place the dough in an oiled bowl, turning the ball to coat it with oil. Cover and let rise in a warm, draft-free place for about 1 hour, until doubled in bulk.

4. Divide the dough into two balls. Brush two baking sheets or pizza pans with oil. Stretch one ball of dough to fit each pan. The dough is now ready for topping with sauce and vegetables.

TASTY TOFU AND TEMPEH

Soy-Glazed Tofu

Slow-Roasted Sesame Tofu

Hoisin-Roasted Tofu

Barbecue-Style Roasted Tempeh

Lettuce-Wrapped Tempeh in Chinese Brown Sauce

Lettuce-Wrapped Tempeh in Chinese Hoisin Sauce

Soy-Glazed Tofu

SERVES 4 TO 6

CAN YOU EVER have enough recipes for enjoying tofu? This one is very easy—a no-brainer. The roasted tofu is tasty enough to eat as it is—my kids will snack on roasted tofu straight out of the refrigerator. It also makes a superior base for a feast of roasted mushrooms—just pile the mushrooms on top of the roasted tofu. You can also cut the tofu into cubes and add them to a stir-fry.

2 pounds extra-firm or firm tofu
1 tablespoon soy sauce
1 tablespoon toasted sesame oil or peanut oil

1. Preheat the oven to 425°F. Lightly oil a rimmed baking sheet.

2. Wrap the tofu in paper towels and squeeze gently to remove excess moisture. Cut each block horizontally into three ½-inch-thick slices.

3. Combine the soy sauce and oil and brush on both sides of the tofu slices. Arrange on the baking sheet.

4. Roast for about 15 minutes, until lightly browned on both sides, turning once.

5. Serve hot.

Slow-Roasted Sesame Tofu

SERVES 4 TO 6

BY SLOW-ROASTING the tofu, you give it time to absorb all the delicious marinade. This tofu can be served as a topping for rice, but I prefer it at room temperature, as an hors d'oeuvre, snack, or lunch box treat.

2 pounds extra-firm or firm tofu

6 tablespoons soy sauce

¼ cup dry sherry or rice wine

3 tablespoons toasted sesame oil

2 tablespoons rice vinegar

1 tablespoon plus 1 teaspoon sugar

2 garlic cloves, minced

½ to 1 teaspoon Chinese chili paste with garlic (available where Chinese foods are sold)

3 tablespoons white (hulled) sesame seeds

1. Preheat the oven to 350°F. Lightly oil a 9 x 13-inch baking dish.

2. Wrap the tofu in paper towels and squeeze gently to remove excess moisture. Cut each block horizontally into three ½-inch-thick slices. Cut each slice in half, then cut each half into 2 triangles. Arrange in a single snug layer in the baking dish.

3. Combine the soy sauce, sherry, oil, vinegar, sugar, garlic, and chili paste in a small bowl and whisk to combine. Pour over the tofu.

4. Roast for 30 minutes. Turn the tofu over, scatter the sesame seeds on top, and roast for about another 15 minutes, until the marinade has been mostly absorbed and the sesame seeds are very lightly colored.

5. Serve hot or at room temperature. The tofu can be refrigerated in an airtight container for 4 to 5 days.

Hoisin-Roasted Tofu

ROASTED TOFU CAN take the place of meat on the dinner plate. It is all protein and very satisfying, especially with the tangy, sweet glaze and crunchy peanut topping here. Accompany the tofu with rice and stir-fried broccoli for a simple, deliciously nutritious dinner.

2 pounds extra-firm or firm tofu

¼ cup hoisin sauce

¼ cup dry sherry or rice wine

2 tablespoons soy sauce

2 tablespoons sugar

2 garlic cloves, minced

¼ cup finely chopped dry-roasted peanuts

1. Preheat the oven to 350°F. Lightly oil a 9 x 13-inch baking dish.

2. Wrap the tofu in paper towels and squeeze gently to remove excess moisture. Cut each block horizontally into three ½-inch-thick slices. Cut each slice in half, then cut each half into 2 triangles. Arrange in a single snug layer in the baking dish.

3. Combine the hoisin sauce, sherry, soy sauce, sugar, and garlic in a small bowl and whisk to combine. Pour about three-quarters of the sauce over the tofu.

4. Roast for 30 minutes. Turn the tofu over, brush with the remaining sauce, and scatter the peanuts on top. Roast for about another 15 minutes, until the sauce has been mostly absorbed and the peanuts are very lightly colored.

5. Serve hot or at room temperature. The tofu can be refrigerated in an airtight container for 4 to 5 days.

Barbecue-Style Roasted Tempeh

SERVES 4 TO 6

MY FIRST INTRODUCTION to tempeh was in scrambled eggs—and it was another twenty years before I gave tempeh a second chance. Tempeh is a fermented soybean cake with a nutty, yeasty flavor. Most people think the yeasty flavor needs taming, so they prefer to mask it with a strongly flavored sauce. This barbecue-flavored tempeh is delicious served on its own, but I also love to sandwich it between slices of toasted whole wheat bread.

---

1 cup ketchup

2 tablespoons cider, malt, or red wine vinegar

1 tablespoon plus 1 teaspoon soy sauce

2 tablespoons sugar

2 tablespoons chili powder

½ to 1 teaspoon ground chipotle chile

2 garlic cloves, minced

16 ounces soy tempeh, cut into ½-inch-wide strips

1. Preheat the oven to 350°F. Lightly oil an 8- or 9-inch baking dish.

2. In a small bowl, combine the ketchup, vinegar, soy sauce, sugar, chili powder, chipotle, and garlic. Whisk to combine. Taste and adjust the seasonings, if needed.

3. Pour half the sauce into the baking dish. Arrange the tempeh on top in a single layer. Pour the remaining sauce on top. Using a brush or wooden spoon, distribute the sauce so that the tempeh is completely covered.

4. Roast for about 30 minutes, until the sauce is mostly absorbed.

5. Serve hot or at room temperature.

Lettuce-Wrapped Tempeh in Chinese Brown Sauce

SERVES 4 TO 6

I WAS NEWLY INFATUATED with tempeh and looking for new flavor combinations when I first roasted tempeh in a fairly traditional sauce made with Chinese oyster sauce. The tempeh was good on its own, but something prompted me to wrap it in a lettuce leaf with scallions and cucumber. Heaven! It makes a wonderful meal accompanied by fried rice.

¾ cup high-quality neutral-tasting chicken or vegetable broth

6 tablespoons oyster sauce (see Note on page 12)

¼ cup soy sauce

2 tablespoons dry sherry or rice wine

2 teaspoons toasted sesame oil

2 tablespoons cornstarch

1 tablespoon peeled and minced fresh ginger

2 teaspoons sugar

4 garlic cloves, minced

16 ounces soy tempeh

2 to 3 heads Boston, butter, or romaine lettuce, separated into individual leaves

1 bunch (8 to 12) scallions, thinly sliced lengthwise and cut into 3-inch lengths

1 English cucumber, thinly sliced lengthwise and cut into 3-inch lengths

1. Preheat the oven to 350°F. Lightly oil a 9 x 13-inch baking dish.

2. In a small bowl, combine the broth, oyster sauce, soy sauce, sherry, oil, cornstarch, ginger, sugar, and garlic. Whisk to combine. Pour half the sauce into the baking dish. Cut the tempeh in half horizontally. Then cut each half into ½-inch-wide strips. Arrange in a single layer in the baking dish. Pour the remaining sauce on top.

3. Roast for about 30 minutes, until the sauce is mostly absorbed, turning once about halfway through.

4. To serve, arrange the tempeh, lettuce, scallions, and cucumber on a serving platter. Place a piece of tempeh in a lettuce leaf, add a few pieces of scallion and cucumber, fold into a bite-size package, and eat.

Lettuce-Wrapped Tempeh in Chinese Hoisin Sauce

SERVES 4 TO 6

THIS IS A VARIATION on the previous recipe, but it's such a strong family favorite that I could not choose between the two.

¾ cup high-quality neutral-tasting chicken or vegetable broth

½ cup hoisin sauce

2 tablespoons soy sauce

2 tablespoons dry sherry or rice wine

1 tablespoon peeled and minced fresh ginger

4 garlic cloves, crushed

16 ounces soy tempeh

2 to 3 heads Boston, butter, or romaine lettuce, separated into individual leaves

1 bunch (8 to 12) scallions, thinly sliced lengthwise and cut into 3-inch lengths

1 English cucumber, thinly sliced lengthwise and cut into 3-inch lengths

1. Preheat the oven to 350°F. Lightly oil a 9 x 13-inch baking dish.

2. In a small bowl, combine the broth, hoisin sauce, soy sauce, sherry, ginger, and garlic. Whisk to combine.

3. Pour half the sauce into the baking dish. Cut the tempeh in half horizontally. Cut each half into ½-inch-wide strips. Arrange in a single layer in the baking dish. Pour the remaining sauce on top.

4. Roast for about 30 minutes, until the sauce is mostly absorbed, turning once about halfway through.

5. To serve, arrange the tempeh, lettuce, scallions, and cucumber on a serving platter. Place a piece of tempeh in a lettuce leaf, add a few pieces of scallion and cucumber, fold into a bite-size package, and eat.

GREAT GRAINS, NUTS, AND SEEDS

Spiced Mixed Nuts

Roasted Chestnuts

Tamari-Roasted Sunflower Seeds

Chili-Roasted Pepitas

Honey-Pecan Granola

Blueberry Sunrise Granola

Amazing Almond Granola

Apple Crisp Granola

Tropical Paradise Granola

Cashew Crunch Granola

Maple Morning Granola

Worth-the-Hike Trail Mix

Spiced Mixed Nuts

TO WATCH YOUR FRIENDS attack a bowl of nuts is to watch their true personalities emerge. Do they fish out the pecans and leave the peanuts behind? Or do your friends grab the nuts by the handful and pop them all in their mouths at once—going for the full flavor, the big sensation? Or are they unusually fair-minded individuals who take a handful but eat the nuts one by one, the peanuts penance for the pecans? Well, you could make a batch of nuts that includes only the crowd pleasers—pecans, cashews, hazelnuts, and almonds—but I think a few peanuts keep us all humble.

4 cups mixed nuts, such as almonds, Brazil nuts, cashews, hazelnuts, peanuts, pecans, and walnuts

¼ cup (½ stick) butter, melted

2 tablespoons coarse sea salt or kosher salt

2 tablespoons sugar

1 to 2 teaspoons chili powder

¼ teaspoon ground cinnamon

1. Preheat the oven to 350°F. Line a large roasting pan or half sheet pan with parchment paper.

2. Blanch the nuts in a large pot of boiling water for 1 minute. Drain well.

3. In a large bowl, combine the drained nuts with the butter, salt, sugar, chili powder, and cinnamon. Toss to coat well. Spread out in a shallow (preferably single) layer in the pan.

4. Roast for about 20 minutes, until the nuts are fragrant and lightly colored, stirring or shaking the pan occasionally for even cooking.

5. Transfer to a large bowl and let cool completely. The nuts will become crisp as they cool.

6. Store in an airtight jar for up to 1 week at room temperature or for several months in the refrigerator.

Roasted Chestnuts

LOOK FOR IMPORTED CHESTNUTS during the winter holiday season. The aroma of roasting chestnuts adds a festive touch to any gathering.

1 pound chestnuts

1. Preheat the oven to 450°F.

2. With the tip of a sharp knife, score the flat side of each nut with an X. Arrange in a single layer on a baking sheet.

3. Roast for about 15 minutes, until the peel separates easily from the nut, shaking the pan occasionally for even cooking.

4. Serve immediately. The chestnuts are much easier to peel while they are still warm.

Toasting Nuts and Seeds Toasting nuts and seeds is essential for bringing out their flavor and making their texture delightfully crunchy. For a small quantity, it is best to put them in a dry skillet over medium heat. Toast, stirring the nuts or shaking the pan, just until they begin to release their fragrance and take on a slightly darker color, about 4 minutes. Watch carefully and be prepared to remove the nuts as soon as they are ready. If they are allowed to become too dark, their flavor will be bitter and scorched. Large quantities can be spread out on a baking sheet and toasted in a 325°F oven for 5 to 7 minutes. Be sure to check and stir often.

Tamari-Roasted Sunflower Seeds

WARNING! THESE SUNFLOWER seeds are highly addictive. Do not attempt this recipe unless you have a good stock of beer to go with them or your self-control is firmly in hand. To those with self-control, I might add that these sunflower seeds make a wonderful addition to salads, especially spinach salad dressed with a soy vinaigrette.

2 cups hulled sunflower seeds
¼ cup tamari or soy sauce

1. Preheat the oven to 300°F. Line a baking sheet with parchment paper or lightly oil the sheet.

2. Combine the sunflower seeds and tamari in a medium-size bowl. Toss to coat well. Spread out on the baking sheet.

3. Roast for 15 to 20 minutes, scraping the seeds off the paper with a spatula and stirring well about halfway through, until the seeds are lightly browned and the tamari is all absorbed. Check frequently during the last 5 minutes to prevent scorching.

4. Transfer to a medium-size bowl to cool completely. The seeds will become crisp as they cool.

5. Store in an airtight jar for up to 1 week at room temperature or for up to 1 month in the refrigerator.

Chili-Roasted Pepitas

MAKES 2 CUPS

ROASTED PUMPKIN SEEDS are every bit as addictive as roasted sunflower seeds, so take care when making and serving these. You can buy pumpkin seeds in health food stores, but you can also roast the seeds from any pumpkin you happen to have on hand. Just wash the seeds in a bowl of water to separate them from the stringy fibers to which they are attached, then pat dry with paper towels. You can season the seeds with a good commercial chili powder (which is made from dried chiles plus other seasonings, such as Mexican oregano) or pure ground chiles.

3 cups hulled pumpkin seeds

3 tablespoons peanut, canola, or olive oil

1 tablespoon chili powder or pure ground chile

1 teaspoon salt

1 teaspoon ground cumin

1. Preheat the oven to 300°F. Line a baking sheet with parchment paper or lightly oil the sheet.

2. Place the pumpkin seeds in a medium-size bowl. In a small bowl, combine the oil, chili powder, salt, and cumin and stir well. Pour over the pumpkin seeds and toss to coat well. Spread out in a single layer on the baking sheet.

3. Roast for 25 to 30 minutes, until the seeds are lightly browned and crunchy, stirring or shaking the pan occasionally for even cooking. Check frequently during the last 5 minutes to prevent scorching.

4. Transfer to a medium-size bowl to cool completely. The seeds will become crisp as they cool.

5. Store in an airtight jar for up to 1 week at room temperature or for up to 1 month in the refrigerator.

Honey-Pecan Granola

EVERY TIME I MAKE a new batch of granola, I think, "This is the best granola I've ever made." What I forget between batches is that homemade granola is *so much better* than store-bought because it is so much fresher. The difference in flavor between homemade and store-bought granola is as great as the difference between homemade and supermarket bread. There is no comparison. This particular version is a classic and near-perfect granola. I like fresh sliced bananas in this granola, but adding dried fruit is always an option.

2 cups rolled (old-fashioned) oats

1 cup rolled barley or wheat flakes (available in natural food stores)

1 cup pecan pieces

1 cup raw or toasted wheat germ

¾ teaspoon salt

½ teaspoon ground cinnamon

Pinch of nutmeg

⅓ cup canola or grapeseed oil

½ cup honey

1. Preheat the oven to 300°F. Line a large shallow roasting pan with parchment paper.

2. In a large bowl, combine the oats, barley, pecans, wheat germ, salt, cinnamon, and nutmeg. Mix well.

3. In a large glass measuring cup, combine the oil and honey. Cover and heat in the microwave for about 30 seconds. Or combine in a small saucepan and heat over medium-low heat for a few minutes, until the mixture is quite liquid and warm to the touch. Stir vigorously to combine. Stir into the oat mixture and mix well. Spread out in the pan.

4. Roast for 30 to 45 minutes, until the granola is golden, stirring occasionally for even cooking. Do not let the granola get too dark, and stir frequently during the final 15 minutes to prevent scorching the granola at the sides of the pan. Turn off the heat and leave the granola in the cooling oven for 1 hour. This helps the granola develop a crisp texture, despite the presence of the honey.

5. Transfer to a large bowl to cool completely.

6. Store in an airtight container. Granola will keep for about 1 month at room temperature or for about 6 months in the refrigerator.

Crunchy Granola Granola comes out of the oven disappointingly limp. Don't worry about it—and do not keep roasting, thinking the granola will become crisp; it will simply scorch. The granola will become nicely crunchy as it cools. If you are making granola on an especially humid day, or if the granola seems really, really soft, you can let it cool slowly in the oven with the oven door ajar and the heat off. This will allow any latent moisture to evaporate.

Blueberry Sunrise Granola

MAKES ABOUT 8 CUPS

THE FLAVORS ARE SIMPLE in this basic granola, allowing the rich roasted flavor of pecans and the sweet, summery flavor of blueberries to shine. Dried blueberries are available in natural food stores. They make a welcome change from boring old raisins, but raisins, dried cherries, or chopped dried apples can be substituted.

3 cups rolled (old-fashioned) oats
2 cups chopped pecans
1 cup hulled sunflower seeds
½ cup firmly packed light brown sugar
1 teaspoon salt
⅓ cup canola or grapeseed oil
1 teaspoon pure vanilla extract
2 cups dried blueberries

1. Preheat the oven to 300°F. Line a large shallow roasting pan with parchment paper.

2. In a large bowl, combine the oats, pecans, sunflower seeds, brown sugar, and salt. Mix well. Stir in the oil and vanilla. Spread out in the pan.

3. Roast for 25 to 30 minutes, until the granola is golden, stirring occasionally for even cooking. Do not let the granola get too dark, and stir frequently during the final 15 minutes to prevent scorching the granola at the sides of the pan.

4. Transfer to a large bowl to cool completely. Stir in the blueberries.

5. Store in an airtight container. This will keep for about 1 month at room temperature or for about 6 months in the refrigerator.

Serving Granola Serving homemade granola with skim milk is like serving homemade bread with margarine. Unless you really cannot tolerate the extra fat, give yourself a treat and enjoy your granola with whole milk. I won't even mention how exquisite homemade granola tastes with half-and-half . . . .

Amazing Almond Granola

MAKES ABOUT 6 CUPS

ALMONDS HAVE A VERY distinctive presence in this granola. Mix in dried fruit, if you like; I prefer it with a sliced fresh banana or fresh berries.

2 cups rolled (old-fashioned) oats

1 cup rolled barley or wheat flakes (available in natural food stores)

1 cup slivered almonds

1 cup hulled sunflower seeds

1 cup raw or toasted wheat germ

¾ teaspoon salt

Pinch of nutmeg

⅔ cup pure maple syrup

⅓ cup canola or grapeseed oil

1 teaspoon pure vanilla extract

1 teaspoon pure almond extract

1. Preheat the oven to 300°F. Line a large shallow roasting pan with parchment paper.

2. In a large bowl, combine the oats, barley, almonds, sunflower seeds, wheat germ, salt, and nutmeg. Mix well.

3. In a glass measuring cup, combine the maple syrup and oil. Cover and heat in the microwave for 30 seconds. Or combine in a small saucepan and heat over medium-low heat for a few minutes, until the mixture is quite liquid and warm to the touch. Stir vigorously to combine. Stir in the vanilla and almond extract.

4. Stir the maple mixture into the oat mixture and mix well. Spread out in the pan.

5. Roast for 30 to 45 minutes, until the granola is golden, stirring occasionally for even cooking. Do not let the granola get too dark, and stir frequently during the final 15 minutes to prevent scorching the granola at the sides of the pan.

6. Transfer to a large bowl to cool completely.

7. Store in an airtight container. This will keep for about 1 month at room temperature or for about 6 months in the refrigerator.

Apple Crisp Granola

ALL THE WONDERFUL fall flavors of apple crisp in your bowl of morning cereal. Apple cider baked into the grains and dried apple bits provide a double dose of apple goodness.

2 cups rolled (old-fashioned) oats

1 cup rolled barley or wheat flakes (available in natural food stores)

1 cup walnut pieces

1 cup hulled sunflower seeds

1 cup raw or toasted wheat germ

1 teaspoon salt

1 teaspoon ground cinnamon

¼ teaspoon ground ginger

Pinch of nutmeg

1 cup apple cider

½ cup firmly packed light brown sugar

⅓ cup canola or grapeseed oil

1 cup finely chopped dried apple pieces

1. Preheat the oven to 300°F. Line a large shallow roasting pan with parchment paper.

2. In a large bowl, combine the oats, barley, walnuts, sunflower seeds, wheat germ, salt, cinnamon, ginger, and nutmeg. Mix well.

3. In a small saucepan, bring the cider to a boil. Continue to boil until it becomes syrupy and its volume is reduced by one-half, about 4 minutes. Stir in the brown sugar and oil. Continue to stir until the sugar is melted. Stir the cider mixture into the oat mixture and mix well. Spread out in the pan.

4. Roast for 40 to 45 minutes, until the granola is golden, stirring occasionally for even cooking. Do not let the granola get too dark, and stir frequently during the final 15 minutes to prevent scorching the granola at the sides of the pan.

5. Transfer to a large bowl to cool completely. Mix in the dried apples.

6. Store in an airtight container. This will keep for about 1 month at room temperature or for about 6 months in the refrigerator.

Tropical Paradise Granola

IN THE DEAD OF WINTER, this granola will not replace the tropical vacation you are yearning for, but it surely will delight your taste buds. Dried tropical fruit, such as mangoes or papayas, replace the ubiquitous raisins. Coconut milk is baked into the grains to provide a strong coconut presence. Canned coconut milk is available wherever Latin or Asian foods are sold.

2 cups rolled (old-fashioned) oats

1 cup rolled barley or wheat flakes (available in natural food stores)

1 cup raw or toasted wheat germ

1 cup slivered almonds

¾ cup firmly packed light brown sugar

½ cup unsweetened shredded coconut (available in natural food stores)

1 teaspoon salt

¾ cup unsweetened coconut milk (light can be used)

2 teaspoons pure vanilla extract

1 cup diced dried mangoes, papayas, or dates

1. Preheat the oven to 300°F. Line a large shallow roasting pan with parchment paper.

2. In a large bowl, combine the oats, barley, wheat germ, almonds, brown sugar, coconut, and salt.

3. In a large glass measuring cup, combine the coconut milk and vanilla. Pour into the oat mixture and mix well. Spread out in the baking pan.

4. Roast for about 1 hour, until the granola is golden, stirring occasionally for even cooking. Do not let the granola get too dark, and stir more frequently during the final 15 minutes to prevent scorching the granola at the sides of the pan.

5. Transfer to a large bowl to cool completely. Stir in the dried fruit.

6. Store in an airtight container. This will keep for about 1 month at room temperature or for about 6 months in the refrigerator.

Cashew Crunch Granola

LIGHTLY SWEETENED and sweetly spiced, this reduced-fat granola is a cashew lover's delight. Evaporated skim milk provides the moisture that oil provides in more traditional recipes.

2 cups rolled (old-fashioned) oats

1½ cups raw cashew pieces

1 cup rolled barley or wheat flakes (available in natural food stores)

1 cup raw or toasted wheat germ

¾ cup firmly packed light brown sugar

1 teaspoon ground cinnamon

1 teaspoon salt

¼ teaspoon ground ginger

¼ teaspoon ground allspice

Pinch of nutmeg

¾ cup evaporated skim milk

2 teaspoons pure vanilla extract

1 cup dried cherries, berries, raisins, or currants

1. Preheat the oven to 300°F. Line a large shallow roasting pan with parchment paper.

2. In a large bowl, combine the oats, cashews, barley, wheat germ, brown sugar, cinnamon, salt, ginger, allspice, and nutmeg.

3. In a large glass measuring cup, combine the evaporated milk and vanilla. Pour into the oat mixture and mix well. Spread out in the pan.

4. Roast for 45 to 50 minutes, until the granola is golden, stirring occasionally for even cooking. Do not let the granola get too dark, and stir frequently during the final 15 minutes to prevent scorching the granola at the sides of the pan.

5. Transfer to a large bowl to cool completely. Stir in the dried fruit.

6. Store in an airtight container. This will keep for about 1 month at room temperature or for about 6 months in the refrigerator.

Maple Morning Granola

ALL THE REASON you need to get up in the morning. A subtle blend of sweet spices, cranberries, and maple syrup gives this granola outstanding flavor.

---

3 cups rolled (old-fashioned) oats

1 cup raw or toasted wheat germ

1 cup hulled sunflower seeds

1 cup walnut pieces

1 teaspoon salt

1 teaspoon ground cinnamon

1 teaspoon ground ginger

Pinch of nutmeg

Pinch of ground cloves

¾ cup pure maple syrup

⅓ cup canola or grapeseed oil

1½ teaspoons pure vanilla extract

2 cups dried cranberries or raisins

1. Preheat the oven to 300°F. Line a large shallow roasting pan with parchment paper.

2. In a large bowl, combine the oats, wheat germ, sunflower seeds, walnuts, salt, cinnamon, ginger, nutmeg, and cloves. Mix well.

3. In a large glass measuring cup, combine the maple syrup and oil. Cover and heat in the microwave for about 30 seconds. Or combine in a small saucepan and heat over medium-low heat for a few minutes, until the mixture is quite liquid and warm to the touch. Stir vigorously to combine. Stir in the vanilla.

4. Stir the syrup mixture into the oat mixture and mix well. Spread out in the pan.

5. Roast for 35 to 40 minutes, until the granola is golden, stirring occasionally for even cooking. Do not let the granola get too dark, and stir frequently during the final 15 minutes to prevent scorching the granola at the sides of the pan.

6. Transfer to a large bowl to cool completely. Stir in the cranberries.

7. Store in an airtight container. This will keep for about 1 month at room temperature or for about 6 months in the refrigerator.

Parchment Paper Saves Cleanup Granola will stick to the roasting pan unless you oil the pan or line it with parchment paper. Both work well to prevent sticking, but I prefer the parchment paper because it makes cleanup much easier. Also, by lifting the paper up at the sides of the pan, you can easily move the granola away from the edges if overbrowning starts to become a problem.

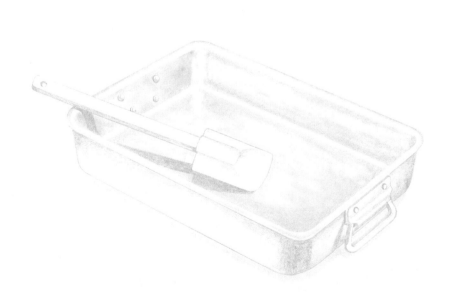

Worth-the-Hike Trail Mix

MAKES ABOUT 12 CUPS

THEORETICALLY, THIS MIXTURE will keep for about 1 month at room temperature or for about 6 months in the refrigerator—but I have not been able to fully test this out, for obvious reasons. You can play around with the ingredients, using different nuts or different dried fruit, or you can substitute M&M's for some or all of the chocolate chips. The corn syrup is essential for creating clusters of nuts and oats.

3 cups rolled (old-fashioned) oats

2 cups walnut pieces

1 cup pecan pieces

1 cup hulled sunflower seeds

1 teaspoon salt

½ cup light or golden corn syrup

⅓ cup canola or grapeseed oil

¼ cup firmly packed light brown sugar

1 teaspoon pure vanilla extract

One 12-ounce bag (2 cups) semisweet chocolate morsels

1 cup raisins

1 cup dried cherries or cranberries

1. Preheat the oven to 300°F. Line a large shallow roasting pan with parchment paper.

2. In a large bowl, combine the oats, walnuts, pecans, sunflower seeds, and salt. Mix well.

3. In a large glass measuring cup, combine the corn syrup, oil, and brown sugar. Cover and heat in the microwave for about 30 seconds. Or combine in a small saucepan and heat over medium-low heat for a few minutes, until the mixture is quite liquid and warm to the touch. Stir in the vanilla.

4. Stir the syrup mixture into the oat mixture and mix well. Spread out in the pan.

5. Roast for about 40 minutes, until the mix is golden, stirring occasionally for even cooking. Do not let the mix get too dark, and stir frequently during the final 15 minutes to prevent scorching the mix at the sides of the pan.

6. Let the mixture cool undisturbed. As the oats and nuts cool, they will clump together.

7. Break up the mixture into bite-size morsels. Transfer to a large bowl. Mix in the chocolate morsels, raisins, and cherries.

8. Store in an airtight container.

INDEX